GRIT TO GRAPPLE WITH LIFE

LIFE

A.M., D.D.

BROADMAN PRESS
NASHVILLE, TENNESSEE

Printed in the United States of America
1000—3-42—3

TO

FLORENCE WILSON CAMPBELL

DEAR COMPANION AND HELPMATE

THIS VOLUME IS AFFECTIONATELY

DEDICATED

CONTENTS

FOREWORD

Since the recent publication of *Making Marriage Christian* and *The Blessing of Believing,* the very heavy duties and responsibilities of a great church have kept me so completely occupied that I have not had time to write for publication. However, within the past year I have been repeatedly urged by many of my brethren in the ministry to prepare another manuscript.

At last I have yielded to the judgment and the wish of my brethren and now offer GRIT TO GRAPPLE WITH LIFE in the hope that it may furnish some help and encouragement "In the strife of truth with falsehood, for the good or evil side."

I gratefully acknowledge the valuable help which Mrs. Campbell has rendered in reading the manuscript and correcting many mistakes and errors. Furthermore, I wish to acknowledge my indebtedness to others, for, like most writers, I am a part of all that I have ever read.

I wish also to thank Dr. John W. Bradbury for the privilege of including "We Would See Jesus," which in brief appeared in *The Watchman-Examiner,* August 1, 1940.

STROTHER A. CAMPBELL

Baptist Temple
Charleston, West Virginia

I

GRIT TO GRAPPLE WITH LIFE

I have been initiated into the secret for all sorts and conditions of life, . . . in Him who strengthens me, I am able for anything.—PHILIPPIANS 4:12-13 (Moffatt).

I

In these dreadful days of treachery and betrayal on the part of men and nations, even religion and life have their "fifth columns." Before we are aware, the enemy within, posing as a friend, regarded as an ally, has betrayed us, weakened our defense by leaving our left flank unprotected, thus making defeat or retreat inevitable. This sudden and unexpected turn of events has left many sadly disillusioned, baffled, and bewildered. No wonder, then, that many men lack the grit to continue their grapple with life! In recent years not a few have lost their poise and parted with their composure and confidence, not so much because something dreadful has happened without, but because something tragic has gone wrong within.

How is it with you when there is a sudden and an unexpected turn of events? When some contrary circumstance hurls itself against you and bowls you over, what then? Have you the grit to get up and grapple with life in a manly way, or do you whine and whimper and acknowledge defeat? There are not a few who, when frustrated, lose their self-control and burst out in wild rebellion against the unwelcome limitations of life. They wave a red flag of defiance in the face of

defeat by taking to drink, to drug, or to a wilful viola-
tion of the moral law. There are others who, when they
become painfully aware of the fact that life is too difficult for their meager means and puny powers, raise
the ancient Hamletic question,

> To be or not to be: that is the question:
> Whether 'tis nobler in the mind to suffer
> The slings and arrows of outrageous fortune,
> Or to take arms against a sea of trouble,
> And by opposing end them? To die: to sleep;
> No more; and by a sleep to say we end
> The heart-ache and the thousand natural shocks
> That flesh is heir to: 'tis a consummation
> Devoutly to be wish'd. . . .

Alas! not a few foolishly decide "not to be."

If ever you feel like that, listen to this: "I pray
not that thou shouldest take them out of the world, but
that thou shouldest keep them from the evil." No, said
Jesus in his intercessory prayer for the disciples, do not
remove them from the thick of the fight and the press
of the battle. Only give them grit to grapple with
life, sufficient grace to keep "faith sweet and strong,"
and a "trust that triumphs over wrong." Let them bear
the brunt of the battle, but keep them from being soiled
and sullied in spirit and disposition by the things that
happen to them.

The thing that matters most is not the trials and
tribulations with which we must grapple, but the spirit
in which we come to grips with life, and the mood in
which we emerge from the struggle. The manner in
which a man conducts himself while grappling with
life and the condition of his spirit upon emerging are

the real tests of his character. We all admire the man who can come to grips with an evil spirit and yet not allow his own spirit to become evil; who can grapple with mean methods and yet not allow his method to become mean. It is not always ours to choose our antagonist or the field of battle. But it is ours to determine the spirit of the combat and the attitude with which we shall emerge from the ordeal. The history of mankind furnishes ample proof of the thesis that the struggles of life improve personality rather than do violence to it. Therefore, there is no need that, like Saul of old, one should fall on his own sword when the battle goes against him. There is a more excellent way. It is graphically expressed by Moffatt's translation of the valiant words of Paul: "I have been initiated into the secret for all sorts and conditions of life, for plenty and for hunger, for prosperity and for privations; in Him who strengthens me, I am able for anything."

Here was a man who had grit to grapple with life without allowing his spirit to become sullied. He does not claim to have an explanation for all the vicissitudes of life. No, not that at all. But of one thing he does boast: that there had been imparted to him both the grace and the grit to stand up and take anything that life could do to him. He was no pawn nor plaything of circumstances. Strengthened by Christ, he was master of every situation in which he found himself— "able for anything." He had been initiated into a secret which enabled him to triumph gloriously over the worst combination of adverse forces that fate could muster. In the press of the battle with life flinging against him the worst that it could mobilize, he had peace and confidence in his heart, valor in his spirit, and victory for his reward. Yes, says Paul, the power to remain unperturbed in trying days when all things seem to go dead wrong; the ability to face difficulty and disappointment with pulse beating calmly and with a spirit that sees things through to victory with honor —that is the secret which Christ imparted to me. "Not as the world giveth, give I unto you," said Jesus. No, not that at all. I have no earthly goods to offer. I haven't so much as a place to lay my head. But one thing I can bequeath to you: strength to stand the test, courage to carry on, grit to grapple with life and extract victory from apparent defeat.

II

So far, all this may mean nothing more than the preachment of a rather pretty sentiment. What most of us want is not pulpit platitudes, but practice; not declarations, but demonstrations. We'd "rather see a sermon than hear one any day." It is our unqualified conviction that

> The best of all the preachers
>   Are the men who live their creeds;
> For to see good put in action
>   Is what everybody needs.

The question that comes to mind is, Is this a mere pulpit platitude, or was Paul able to practice what he preached? The answer is that the life of the preacher was one continuous and glorious demonstration of the truth which he declared. Now and then he made the truth which he proclaimed stand up like a towering peak in a great mountain range. Take, for example, his ex-

perience in the city of Philippi where he was violently
arrested, brutally beaten, wickedly and unjustly condemned and cast into the inner prison and his feet made
fast in the stocks.   Enough to subdue the spirit and
silence the voice of a mere proclaimer of platitudes!
But not so with the Apostle Paul.   Here was a man
to whom God had given sufficient grace and grit to
grapple with life even when the odds were stacked
against him.   He was the sort of man for whom "Stone
walls do not a prison make, nor iron bars a cage."   He
had been initiated into the secret for all sorts and conditions of life.   In Christ who strengthened him, he
was able for anything.   Thus in grappling with a formidable foe, Paul made use of a "secret weapon" of
which his enemy had no knowledge.   At midnight he
prayed, and as a result the doors of the dungeon into
which he was cast were opened, and the bands with
which he was bound were loosed, and he was a free man.

Witness again how convincingly the preacher practiced what he preached as he faced a most harassing
and distressing experience while on his voyage to Rome.
For fourteen days and nights the ship on which he was
a prisoner passenger had been subjected to the merciless
Euroclydon, a storm that took heart and hope out of
every man on board except one, and that one man was
Paul.   Thus again fronted with formidable forces with
which other men had neither the strength nor the courage to grapple, Paul demonstrated the truth that he had
been initiated into the secret for all sorts and conditions of life; that he had a source of strength that made
him able for anything.   He was not the sort of man who
denies the existence of difficulties.   He was no blind

optimist. Neither did he look at the world through rose-colored glasses. No one familiar with his career would think for a moment that he was "carried to the skies on flowery beds of ease." Without flinching he came to grips with stark, stern reality; and in an hour when confidence, courage, and strength had gone from other men, and all hope that they would be saved was taken away, Paul stood up and said, "Sirs, be of good cheer, for I believe God."

A third incident in which he made practice stand up like Pikes Peak in the great Rocky range was during his imprisonment in Rome. To any ordinary man such a frustration of life's work would have been sufficient cause to languish and die in despair. But not so with Paul. He seized the pen and began to write his immortal letters. The prison in which he was incarcerated has long since disappeared, but the product of his pen endures. What a loss it would have been to the world if imperial Rome had been able to shackle his faith as well as his feet! But because he had been initiated into the secret that gave him grit to grapple with a foe as formidable as the Roman Empire, he was able to transmute his prison house into a printing press. The product of his pen not only prevailed over the prison, it vanquished the Roman Empire as well. The word was mightier than the sword.

There is yet another question many of us would like to ask the preacher who declared that he was able for anything: Was he able to practice what he preached "In that last sad hour when we stand alone where the powers of death combine"? How did he acquit himself when faced by the last enemy, the grim "reaper whose name is death"?   Did he lose his poise and part with his composure?   Did his confidence and courage fail, or was his strength sufficient for a successful grapple with this last antagonist?   Let him answer for himself: "I am now ready to be offered, and the time of my departure is at hand.   I have fought a good fight, I have finished my course, I have kept the faith: henceforth there is laid up for me a crown of righteousness, which the Lord, the righteous judge, shall give me." Thus he passed on with a song in his heart and victory for his reward.

III

In these difficult days of disillusionment, doubt, and dismay, we need to discover that the same power possessed by Paul is available for us.   We, too, may have sufficient grit to grapple with life in a difficult world of sin and strife.   For the Christ who strengthened Paul and made him able for anything is the same yesterday, today, and forever.

One of the elements of strength in the secret which Christ imparted to Paul was that he always kept him at his best.   Very soon we learn that if we are to stand up and grapple with life successfully we must do so at our very best.   In no other way can we stand up and take the hard blows that life delivers.   Some years ago Jess Willard, the champion of the ring, was knocked off his feet, and counted out of the fight, by what was described as a mere tap on the jaw.   The secret of his defeat lay in the fact that he was not at his best.   He had not been disciplined and hardened for the blows which his opponent was able to deliver.

When we are at our best physically, we are immune to many of the contagious diseases. But once we allow our physical fitness to fall below normal, we become the prey of disease. This is no less true of the moral and spiritual man. In an hour of moral slump one is in mortal danger of being overcome and ruined. But so long as one is at his best morally and spiritually, he is immune to the attacks of both the tempter and the temptress. "My strength is as the strength of ten," said Sir Galahad, "because my heart is pure." That is the reason the Christian has such a tremendous advantage in his grapple with life. His strength is as the strength of ten because he has One on his side who keeps him at his best—One to whom all power has been given both in heaven and on earth. I am able to stand up and take anything that life can do for me, said Paul, because Christ keeps me at my best and makes up to me the strength I lack.

Moreover, on being initiated into the marvelous mystery of the saving and sustaining grace of Christ, Paul came into possession of adequate resources for his grapple with life. One of the most frequent causes of dismay and defeat is the paralyzing fear that our resources may not be adequate for the exacting requirements of a complex and difficult world. The fear of inadequate resources gives one an inferiority complex and keeps many an otherwise capable person to the low level of mediocrity. But when one faces life with the added strength which Christ imparts, one has a feeling that no matter what happens he will be able to say, "I am able for anything, because I have been initiated into the secret for all sorts and conditions of life." This was the secret of the prophet's confidence when he declared, "They that wait upon the Lord shall renew their strength; they shall mount up with wings as eagles; they shall run, and not be weary; and they shall walk, and not faint." In a day when the demands of life drain to the dregs the resources of men, no one has more graphically expressed the peace which the possession of adequate resources gives than Victor Hugo when he admonishes,

> Let us learn like a bird for a moment to take
> Sweet rest on a branch that is ready to break;
> She feels the branch tremble, yet gaily she sings.
> What is it to her? She has wings, she has wings.

A third element of strength in the secret which Christ imparted to Paul was faith: "The just shall live by faith," said he. "Faith," said Josiah Royce, "is an insight of the soul by which one can stand everything that can happen to him." The miracle which faith has so frequently performed is found in the fact that men hitherto defeated and broken have received power to prevail. Without it no man can expect to have the necessary grit with which to grapple with life in this war torn world of sin and strife.

> O for a faith that will not shrink
>   Tho' pressed by every foe,
> That will not tremble on the brink
>   Of any earthly woe!—
>
> .   .   .   .
>
> A faith that shines more bright and clear
>   When tempests rage without;
> That when in danger knows no fear,
>   In darkness feels no doubt.

Faith is not so much that we believe something as it is the very essence by which we live. "The just shall live by faith," declared Habakkuk. At first he thought that man must live by a system of beliefs, and by understanding God's ways with the world. Things, to his notion, were badly out of joint, because of which he was greatly perplexed and critical of the attitude of God. He was impatient for God to break in and set things right. At last he decided to climb up into his watchtower and wait that he might hear what God had to say in reply to his complaint. While he waited the answer came, "The just shall live by faith." It was enough! A new spirit came into his heart and his life was filled with a strength he had not known before. Forthwith we hear him declare, "Although the fig tree shall not blossom, neither shall fruit be in the vines; the labour of the olive shall fail, and the fields shall yield no meat; the flock shall be cut off from the fold, and there shall be no herd in the stalls: yet I will rejoice in the Lord, I will joy in the God of my salvation."

Today many of us are as greatly troubled and perplexed as was Habakkuk, and not without cause. The world is badly upside down. In our hasty and short-sighted view we are likely to conclude that

Careless seems the great Avenger; history's pages but record
One death-grapple in the darkness 'twixt old systems and the Word;
Truth forever on the scaffold, Wrong forever on the throne.[1]

At times we grow impatient and boldly presume to tell God how to run the universe. It is much easier to

[1] From *American Poets and Their Theology*, by A. H. Strong. Used by permission of The Judson Press, Philadelphia.

tell him what he should do than it is for us to "heed
what he sayeth, do what he willeth." This was the
mood and the attitude which at one time laid its wither-
ing hand on the spirit of Martin Luther and brought
him near the brink of despair. He had almost lost his
grit to grapple with life. While in this sad frame of
mind, Mrs. Luther did an unusual thing. She appeared
before him dressed in deep mourning. When Luther
looked up and saw her in her strange attire, he inquired
the reason for her absurd behavior. She replied, "God
is dead and I am mourning his decease." "Nonsense!"
shouted Luther, "God is not dead." Thereupon he
plunged into an argument to prove that he was still very
much alive. Then it was that Mrs. Luther brought
home to her fretted husband the lesson of her strange
parable. Said she, "From the way you were acting, I
thought God must be dead and you were running the
universe for him." Luther was not slow in learning the
lesson. Like Habakkuk and Paul, he, too, came to realize that "the just shall live by faith." Strengthened
and sustained by his faith in the fact that God was still
alive, he began a grapple with life that made him the
father of the Reformation.

The colossal issues with which the whole human race
must come to grips today are social, political, and religious. Or, to state it another way, the antagonists
with which humanity must grapple are the sinister
ideologies which have come into being because of maladjusted social and economic conditions. These ideologies would pillage and destroy every vestige of human
rights: all the precious possessions bequeathed to us by
our forefathers who fought, bled, and died that we

might be free from tyranny and oppression. If these pagan ideologies prevail, we shall lose our political freedom, our freedom of speech, the freedom of the press, and our religious liberty, and become mere pawns of the state.

No one can be aware of what is going on in the world today and not realize that we are living in a veritable madhouse. The world has broken loose from its moral and mental moorings and is drifting rapidly toward the brink of destruction. In these perilous times when there is danger that civilization may be destroyed and paganism, brutality, and savagery may become the standards of men and nations, we need above all the gift which Christ alone can impart—the gift he bequeathed to Paul: grit to grapple with life.

> God give us grit
>   To grapple with life,
> In a difficult world
>   Of sin and strife.
>
> God give us grit
>   That we may stand
> In a world war torn
>   In many a land.
>
> In a world that calls
>   For wisdom and power,
> God give us grit
>   For this dark hour.
>
> God give us grit
>   That we may stand
> Firm for the right
>   In our native land.

God give us grit
  That we may be
Strong, brave and true
  For home and Thee.

God give us grit,
  Grace, wisdom and power,
To face life's problems
  In this troubled hour.

II

WE WOULD SEE JESUS

Sir, we would see Jesus.—JOHN 12:21.

I

These words voice the urgent request of men who had journeyed from the land of philosophers. They were men whose heads were full of learning, but whose hearts were full of yearning—a yearning which philosophy could not satisfy. They were possessed of a heart hunger which Christ alone could cure.

A similar hunger haunts the hearts of men today. There is a stir of something strange moving through the world. A nameless, indescribable, indefinable something has laid its devastating hand on man, leaving him sadly disillusioned, baffled, bewildered, and hungry of heart. Suddenly humanity has become fluid; or, as General Jan Christian Smuts expressed it, "Humanity has struck its tents and is on the march." But the disquieting thing about it is that humanity seems to be on the march back to paganism, to barbarism, to brutality and savagery. We have well-nigh gained control over nature, but have almost lost control over human nature. The beast of the forest and the field has been subdued; but the brute in man has been unleashed. The civilization which we have builded with our brawn and brain threatens to become our Frankenstein, to turn, rend, and destroy us. It looks as though this age has been inoculated with a virus that has dethroned reason, destroyed moral responsibility, and driven judgment to brutish beasts.

However, all this outward manifestation is but a symptom of something that is inward, something that is hinted and hidden. Whether man is aware of it or not, he is strangely heart hungry. And not understanding just what it is that gives him a sickening sense of always being turned away empty, he hurries from this to that with rapidity and bewildering stupidity only to find that his sense of unsatisfaction has been multiplied and intensified, and his last state worse than the first. An intelligent and cultured gentleman asked for an interview with his pastor. He began by saying: "I do not know what ails me. I have health and I have wealth. I have my family and I have my friends, yet I am wretchedly unhappy. The way I live is so unsatisfying." This man's case is typical of multitudes of men today. They are sick at heart and hungry of soul. Like the Greeks of old, they would see Jesus, the satisfying Saviour.

II

Anyone who has been aware of the trend of religious thought during the past twenty years or more knows full well that the present bewilderment and deep sense of heart hunger have their antecedents. Every effect has its cause. Permit me to sketch the things which in my humble judgment have brought man to his present plight and to his profound sense of unsatisfaction.

When I was a student in the Seminary the so-called "New Theology" was having its day. It was ushered in by a form of biblical study known as "Higher Criticism." The method was much like that of a botanist who sets about to study a beautiful flower. He tears away the corolla and destroys the calyx that he may study the stamen. Such a process may yield some valuable information for the botanist, but it is ruinous to the flower. When he is through with it all the king's oxen and all the king's men cannot put the beautiful flower together again. Even so, higher criticism may have yielded some valuable information for the scholar, but it undermined the faith of the average man and destroyed his confidence in the validity of the Bible as the authoritative word of God. All this in the name of scholarship! But we are beginning to learn that much of that which parades as scholarship is nothing more than scoffership—the prattle of intellectual pagans. It was Voltaire, the atheist, who said, "If we would destroy the Christian religion we must first of all destroy man's belief in the Bible." Thus having taken from man the Bread of Life and having given him a stone instead, is it any wonder that he is so strangely hungry of heart today?

Following the devastating results of Higher Criticism came "Modernism," which, not content with the destruction of man's belief in the Bible as the authoritative word of God, centered its attack on the person and deity of Jesus Christ. IIis divinity was denied and his vicarious atonement derided and discarded. Not by atheists, infidels, and avowed enemies of Jesus Christ, but by teachers in some of our colleges, universities, and theological seminaries, and by men who, like John the Baptist, were divinely sent to say to sinful men, "Behold the Lamb of God, which taketh away the sin of the world."

Last June, in an address before a divisional convention of the American Association for the Advancement of Science, Dr. S. J. Holmes, zoologist, educator, and author, is reported to have said that the Christian code of ethics is not suited to humans in our modern age because it is in conflict with human nature and therefore responsible for some of the world's welfare problems. Certainly the Christian code of ethics has been and always will be in conflict with a materialistic and mechanistic biological interpretation of man which would make virtues out of the brutal and beastly elements in human nature. But because the Christian code of ethics is in conflict with the worst that there is in human nature, he suggests that we discard it for the Darwinian code which "accepts cruelty, lust, deceit, cowardice, and selfishness as intrinsic virtues." Whole nations have done just what Dr. Holmes suggests. With a vengeance they are practicing the vicious brand of philosophy of life which he preaches, and the result is a barbarous and brutal paganism.

What the intellectual pagans who occupy favored places in our colleges, seminaries, and universities fail to realize is that the ethical principles of Christ are responsible for bringing civilization to its highest level, and that these same principles are now preventing the whole world from reverting to barbarism, brutality, and savagery. Man needs and must have something higher than the Darwinian code of ethics, "the code of cruelty, lust, deceit, cowardice, and selfishness as intrinsic virtues."

> A man's reach should exceed his grasp,
> Or what's a heaven for?

It is the virtue of Christianity to transform human nature instead of conforming to it.

As might be expected, following Modernism came the prophets and preachers of "Humanism." At last we were brought to the inevitable: a religion without God. To the humanist the Bible is a code of ethics, God a creation of primitive fears, Jesus Christ no more than a man, and faith a figment of the mind arising out of wistful thinking.

Paralleling the downward drift of religion was a vicious and salacious psychology. One of its chief exponents was the late Sigmund Freud. Such vagaries as free love, or more correctly speaking, a free and unrestrained indulgence of the sex impulse, were advocated. A few years ago, in a former pastorate, one of my fine laymen, a deacon, was indicted in Federal Court for sending salacious literature through the mail. He had copied passages from a book which was being used at the state college located near by and sent them to ministers and leading laymen throughout the state. It was for this that the advocates of academic freedom sought and secured his indictment. But when he came up for trial the case was thrown out of court on the ground that his motive was not to disseminate salacious literature, but to suppress it and prevent its being taught to the youth of the state. But the point I wish to make is that while Higher Criticism, Modernism, and Humanism were busy destroying our faith in the Bible, denying the deity of Jesus Christ, and bringing us at last to a religion without God, certain psychologists were busy completing the work of destruction by undertaking to make moral degenerates of us all. Thus, today we are reaping what we have sown. We sowed to the wind and we are reaping the whirlwind. We sowed to the flesh and we are reaping corruption in high places and low and in between.

III

It has been said, "If man did not have a God, of necessity, he would invent one; for man is instinctively and incurably religious." No tribe or nation, however primitive, has ever been found that did not have a god. Often he is nothing more than a crude creation of human hands, an image carved from wood or stone. Therefore, after Humanism had brought us to the plight of a religion without God, the next step was for man to invent a god to take the place of the true and the living God dethroned and discarded by the process which I have just described.

Witness the vicious circle: Higher Criticism undermined man's belief in the Bible as the authoritative word of God; Modernism shattered his faith in the deity of Jesus Christ, the Son of God, the Saviour of the world; Humanism completed the work of destruction by doing away with God; and then certain psychologists added the finishing touches in an attempt to make moral degenerates of us all. Then it was that man began to "invent" gods, or began a return to the gods of his pagan ancestors. Today he is making gods out of men and religions out of political doctrines. A striking example of this trend is to be found in Russia, whose communistic leaders dethroned and discarded God and outlawed the religion of Jesus Christ because it was "the opiate of the people." Now their god is

Joseph Stalin and their religion a dangerous ideology. Well, of one thing we are certain, their new religion has become "the opiate of the people": multitudes of them have "fallen on sleep." However, they call it "liquidation."

Another sad and sickening example is to be found in the country which mothered Higher Criticism, the land of Martin Luther, the father of the Reformation. Here we see a people deifying a mongrel man and making a religion of a political philosophy. Their religious depravity is revealed in their effort to rewrite the Bible, substituting the gods of their pagan ancestors for the God of the Jews, and the Father of our Lord.

But why pick on other people? There is evidence that this same pagan tendency is taking place in our own country. Panics and depressions have appeared with a semblance of periodic precision. The chief difference between the depression through which we have been passing and those that have preceded it is that in all former depressions the people turned to God, repented of their sins, found moral and spiritual renewal. But in this depression the people have turned their faces toward Washington and placed their hopes in Uncle Sam, and at the same time have become more prodigal and wicked in their ways. Many have become alarmed over the fact that the Federal Government has taken over more and more power. The trouble does not lie with the Federal Government, but in the fact that we have come to think of Uncle Sam as a sort of Santa Claus from whom we can miraculously get something for nothing,—a god who can make the crops big or small as the occasion may require, and give us prosperity by some miraculous arrangement of the alphabet. We need to recognize that the only true recipe for prosperity was proclaimed by God when, in the long ago, he spoke to Solomon saying: "If my people, which are called by my name, shall humble themselves, and pray, and seek my face, and turn from their wicked ways: then will I hear from heaven, and will forgive their sin, and will heal their land."

IV

We are all aware of our impotence today, our inability to cope with difficult circumstances, rapidly changing conditions, and the vicissitudes of life. In spite of our boasted mastery over nature we have a sinking, sickening sense of helplessness and futility. But is it not a significant fact that an era which is characterized by bewilderment, impotence, and futility should be the one which has largely lost its faith, neglected the Bible, denied the deity of Jesus Christ, and turned away from God and the church? Sooner or later we pay for our irreligion and irreverence, and we pay dearly. For it is religion that gives men reason for living, purpose in life, and power to see it through with honor.

Our forefathers faced greater odds than we are called upon to front, yet they knew little or nothing of the sense of impotence and futility which characterizes our day and generation. It was because they possessed a faith that would not shrink, though pressed by every foe, that would not tremble on the brink of any earthly woe. But with us the lamentable thing about it all is that in a day of storm and stress, a day in which there is tragedy on land and sea and in the air, we have well-nigh abandoned the only

> . . . Anchor that keeps the soul,
> Steadfast and sure while the billows roll.

For the dilemmas of life the worldly wise have proposed one exit after another; and we have been willing victims only to find that we have been brought to a dead-end alley. When all else has been tried, maybe we shall come to the conviction voiced by Peter who, in a day when it appeared that all were about to forsake Jesus and turn back to the ways of the world, said: "Lord, to whom shall we go? thou hast the words of eternal life. And we believe and are sure that thou art that Christ, the Son of the living God." For there is no cure for our hopelessness, no satisfaction for our heart hunger, no balm for our sin-sick souls except Jesus. In him we have a well of living water that shall never fail to satisfy, a well that shall never go dry even in extreme drought. "Whosoever drinketh of the water that I shall give him shall never thirst; but the water that I shall give him shall be in him a well of water springing up into everlasting life."

> I heard the voice of Jesus say,
>   "Behold, I freely give
> The living water; thirsty one,
>   Stoop down and drink, and live."
>
> I came to Jesus and I drank
>   Of that life-giving stream;
> My thirst was quenched, my soul revived,
>   And now I live in Him.

Robert Louis Stevenson tells of an exciting experience that befell his grandfather while at sea. The ship on which he was a passenger was caught in a storm and was being driven toward the rocky coast and to certain destruction. When the storm was fiercest he climbed up on deck to face the worst. There he saw the pilot lashed to the wheel, and with might and main he was steering the vessel off the rocks into safer waters. As he stood there watching, the pilot looked up and smiled. It was enough! The smiling face of the pilot was so reassuring that he went back to his cabin saying to himself, "We shall come through, for I saw the face of the pilot and he smiled." What we need desperately in these troubled days is to see the face of our Pilot, the Captain of our salvation.

> We would see Jesus—for the shadows lengthen
>   Across this little landscape of our life;
> We would see Jesus, our weak faith to strengthen,
>   For the last weariness—the final strife.

V

Aware of a strange hunger, the cause of which they do not always understand, multitudes are running about giving themselves without stint to unrestrained indulgence. They are a great deal like the Samaritan woman at the well: life has become so jaded and so unsatisfying that legitimate pleasures no longer suffice. One of the saddest, and yet one of the most illuminating commentaries on this day and generation is that it requires "hot music"—the sort of music which the underworld employs as both a stimulus and an ally to everything that degrades and debauches.

This generation will have to learn again the truth spoken by Jesus to the woman at the well: "Whosoever drinketh of this water shall thirst again: but whosoever drinketh of the water that I shall give him shall never thirst; but the water that I shall give him shall be in him a well of water springing up into everlasting life." Like the prodigal son, we will have to learn that pleasures of the flesh, like wet weather springs, fail in time of drought, fail and leave us with a sinking, sickening sense of being turned away empty.

> Now none but Christ can satisfy,
> None other name for me;
> There's life, and peace, and lasting joy
> Lord Jesus found in thee.

One Sunday morning as he sat in his pulpit, a Boston preacher who had been in the habit of giving his people philosophic essays, book reviews, and literary digests of current events, was handed a note by one of the ushers. The note had been written by a heart-hungry parishioner. When the minister opened the note he read this one crisp sentence, "Sir, we would see Jesus." That should have been sufficient! I wonder if there is not the same sort of heart hunger in the pew today—a heart hunger which looks longingly toward the pulpit saying, "Sir, we would see Jesus." For there is no cure for sin-sick souls, no satisfaction for hungry hearts, no remedy for a war torn world except Jesus Christ.

> Jesus, thou joy of loving hearts,
> Thou fount of life, thou light of men;
> From the best bliss that earth imparts
> We turn unfilled to thee again.

Some years ago the late Rudyard Kipling was very ill. For days he tossed restlessly under a burning fever. As he tossed to and fro he kept mumbling something which no one could quite understand. One morning a nurse bent over him and asked, "Mr. Kipling, what is it you want?" He ceased his restlessness, opened his weary eyes and feebly whispered, "I want God." If we who are called to preach the gospel of Jesus Christ could only understand the incoherent mutterings of this feverish world, and comprehend the unuttered longings of heart-hungry men and women, I think we would hear them saying, "We want God." "Sirs, we would see Jesus."

> We would see Jesus, the great Rock foundation,
>   Whereon our feet were set by sovereign grace;
> Not life, nor death, with all their agitation,
>   Can thence remove us, if we see His face.

III

LIFE'S IRREVOCABLE RECORD

Pilate answered, What I have written I have written.—JOHN 19: 22.

I

Pilate was the Roman ruler before whom Jesus was tried and condemned to die on the cross. "And Pilate wrote a title, and put it on the cross. And the writing was, JESUS OF NAZARETH THE KING OF THE JEWS." The chief priests protested and requested that the title be changed. "Write not," said they, "The King of the Jews; but that he said, I am King of the Jews." With an accent of authority in his voice and a flare of finality in his words Pilate replied, "What I have written I have written."

In his caustic reply Pilate uttered words that were more replete with meaning than he intended. He meant only to remind the Jews that he was a man of authority; that he had the right to write whatever he willed, and the power to declare his action final. But the mistake Pilate made was in thinking that there was finality about what he had written simply because he decreed it to be so. That he had the power to determine his conduct, and the authority to write whatever he willed, we readily admit. But that he had the power to revoke what he had done or to avoid the consequences of his conduct, we readily deny. There was a fixedness and a finality about the act of Pilate apart from the fact that he occupied a place of power which gave his words authority and made his decision final. There was a

[36]

permanency about the words of Pilate which was beyond
the power of Pilate. "What I have written I have
written" was beyond alteration or revocation, not because Pilate said so, but because of the very nature of
his deed. What had been done could not be undone.
There was a finality about his deed that was beyond his
power to cancel or recall. For him it was true that

> The Moving Finger writes; and, having writ,
> Moves on; nor all your Piety nor Wit
> Shall lure it back to cancel half a Line,
> Nor all your Tears wash out a Word of it.

On that day Pilate wrote in the ledger of life a record
that was irrevocable; not because he decreed that it
should be so, but because, in the very nature of things,
it could not be otherwise.

II

These words of Pilate have meaning for us today.
They teach us that there is an element of finality about
the things we do whether we will or no. We have been
making daily entries in the ledger of life; and today
the deep dark truth of Pilate's words stares us in the
face, "What I have written I have written." There is
an element of finality about the daily deeds of the past
which is beyond our ability to alter. Our record is irrevocable.

This fact may be an occasion of comfort to some and
a cause of discomfort, sorrow, and chagrin to others.
It all depends upon what has been written. A few years
ago a minister, with a woman not his wife, registered
in a hotel in a Virginia city. The next morning, on the
way down to the hotel lobby, the elevator stopped at

the floor below and to his amazement and embarrassment a church official of his district stepped in and confronted him. Said the church official, "Introduce me to your friend." In his confusion he denied that he knew her. But the church official knew better. He had been suspected of living a double life and had been trailed. Before leaving, the church official examined the hotel's register and found the telltale evidence. When he was gone, the guilty man approached the hotel clerk and requested the privilege of removing his name from the register; but the clerk refused. "I will give you fifty dollars if you will remove my name from the record," said the sinner. "No," said the clerk, "that is against the rules." "I will give you one hundred dollars," said the guilty man anxiously. "No!" replied the clerk, "that is your record and it must stand just as you made it." Then with a wail he threw up his hands and exclaimed, "My God, I am ruined!" What he had written he had written. And the moving finger having writ moved on; nor all his piety, nor wit could lure it back to cancel half a line; nor all his tears wash out a word of it.

Certainly there is an element of finality about our conduct. Life's record is irrevocable. What we have written we have written. What we are today is the sum total of what we did yesterday. When we take into account the forces which have brought us to our present state, we find that the choices we made and the things we did were the determining factors. Conduct is a very immaterial thing, but it sets us going in a fixed and definite direction and carries us into regions where character is either made or marred. At present we may not quite discern the full truth of this, but in some searching retrospect we shall realize that every choice we made and everything we did was a determining factor in molding our destiny. In the full swing of daily action we may not see all this clearly. Maybe it is well that we do not; for if we should stop to rationalize our conduct we would often paralyze action. But with deepening experience we come to realize that what we have written we have written; and that what we are is the result of what we have done. Therefore, as we look back over our days which are now a part of history, we see with illumined vision the significance of each turn taken and know full well that we are where we are, and what we are, because we went the way we willed to go. We cannot avoid the fact that what we do determines our destiny.

III

Another truth the words of Pilate proclaim to us today is that we are free to make in the ledger of life whatever entries we wish to make. That is the teaching of the Scriptures from Genesis to Revelation. We are free moral agents. "Thus saith the Lord; Behold, I set before you the way of life, and the way of death." The choice belongs to us. However, we must not overlook the fact that freedom of choice carries with it personal responsibility for the results that accrue. No one ever becomes a sinner except by his own consent; and no one ever becomes a saint unless he definitely sets about to become one.

Therefore, as we look back over our transactions, we know full well that all the entries in the ledger of life are in our own handwriting. What we have written we have written. We cannot offer any acceptable alibi. There are some, perhaps, who may be inclined to take refuge behind unfavorable circumstances. But if the Master's parable of the great supper means anything, it teaches that whatever the circumstances may be they cannot be given as a justifiable excuse for not acting the better part. Besides, the best of men have demonstrated this truth for our benefit. No man was more greatly harried by adverse circumstances than the Apostle Paul; but he never gave adversity as an excuse for not achieving for his Lord. Said he: "I know both how to be abased, and I know how to abound: every where and in all things I am instructed both to be full and to be hungry, both to abound and to suffer need." "I have learned, in whatsoever state I am, therewith to be content."

The fact of personal responsibility calls upon us to take a more careful account of inward attitudes and less account of outward circumstances. Freedom of choice places upon us the responsibility of the outcome of our conduct. It shifts the blame from a world which has not been as kind to us as we thought we deserved, to a consideration of the spirit with which we have fronted the world. There may have been many things in the circumstances surrounding our lives in the past which we would have changed if it had been in our power to do so. But the one thing above all else that needed to be altered was our attitude—our sinful selves. Therefore, as we face the future we would do well to pray daily the prayer of the psalmist, "Create in me a clean heart, O God; and renew a right spirit within me." If, like the Apostle Paul, we were fully "initiated into the secret for all sorts and conditions of life," circumstances would not matter nearly so much.

IV

In the next place, the words of Pilate speak to us a message for the present and future as well as for the past. Today we stand at a place of vantage from which we can look to the future as well as to the past. As we review the entries we have made on the leaves of the ledger of life, doubtless there are reasons for regret. We would start a new year with noble resolutions, and for awhile would follow them with good performance. But ere long we had settled back into the same old ways. Now, as we behold our mistakes, they should perform for us the ministry of calling us away from pining over the past to a much better performance henceforth. The mistakes of the past should teach us to deal more wisely with the present and more constructively with the future. What was wrongly done cannot be undone save as out of the doing we may gather a wealth of wisdom that shall help us to act the better part during the days that lie ahead.

However, we should not be allowed to escape the pangs that result from wrongdoing. For it is by means of the remorse of memory and the penalties imposed on misconduct that we are warned and weaned from the wish to walk in the wrong way. Regret over the past is not a pain to be pampered and petted, but a lash to whip our lagging spirits into wiser and nobler action. The spring does not waste her energy lamenting the failure of last autumn's frustrated harvest; she begins again. Even so it should be with us. Past failures should become stimuli to be translated into nobler deeds.

Like the great Apostle Paul, we should forget the things that are behind and, reaching forth unto the things that are before, press on toward the mark for the prize of the high calling of God in Christ Jesus. We are not called upon to reconstruct the past, but to improve the present. Out of past mistakes we should extract the means with which to construct an abiding future.

If, when on a journey, we take the wrong road, we can, with loss of time and temper, go back and take the right road. Not so in the journey of life. We must go on from *where* we are. But we need not go on *as* we are. That is one of the hopes which a new year holds in hand for us; it offers a sort of land of beginning again. Perchance we took the wrong road during the past year. Well, today we stand in the gateway of a new year and can begin to walk in the right way if we will. And "The right way to begin to walk in the right way is to begin right away." The new year will soon slump to the low level of the old unless we match it with newness of life and nobleness of conduct. This we may do if we will; for that is the promise of the gospel of Christ: "If any man be in Christ, he is a new creature: old things are passed away; behold, all things are become new."

Life's record is irrevocable. What we have written we have written. The past is beyond recall. We cannot change nor alter it. But there is One who can cancel the past and blot out our transgressions and remember them no more. He is able to take the leaves of the ledger of life, "sin-stained and blotted," and give us new ones "all unspotted."

Given a new leaf and a new life with which to begin again, we can shape the present and in a large measure determine the future. The past belongs to eternity; but the present belongs to us. We can make of it what we will. Henceforth let us see to it that every entry on the leaves of the ledger of life shall become a record so worthy that there shall be no need nor desire of revoking it; a record that shall merit the Master's "Well done, thou good and faithful servant: . . . enter thou into the joy of thy lord."

THE MAGIC UPLIFT OF THE MORNING UPLOOK

My voice shalt thou hear in the morning, O Lord; in the morning will I direct my prayer unto thee, and will look up.—PSALM 5:3.

I

A great deal depends upon the way in which one begins the day. The mood of the early morning molds the day; the first thought is the tuning fork from which the whole takes its pitch. The psalmist had discovered the right way in which to begin the day: "My voice shalt thou hear in the morning, O Lord; in the morning will I direct my prayer unto thee, and will look up." He had found the magic uplift of the morning uplook.

Man was made to look up. That which distinguishes him from other earthly creatures is his yearning for something higher than either sense or reason can provide. It was Max Muller, a German philosopher, who said, "The ancients derived the word *anthropos* from three Greek words which mean, 'he who looks upward.' " Yet, in spite of the fact that man was made to look up, there are some who have an antipathy for the uplook. Their minds are so completely occupied with material things and earthly pleasures that they have nothing more than the horizontal view. For them life has no perpendiculars, it does not reach up toward God.

There are others who refuse to look up because they deny that there is any *One* to whom they may look.

They are like the ancient professor of Padua who, when Galileo discovered in the blue above Florence the moons of Jupiter, refused to look through the telescope lest he might see that which he refused to believe was there. But his disbelief did not blot out the moons of Jupiter nor any other satellite in the canopy of heaven. Nor has disbelief blotted God out of his universe, though recent years have witnessed a farflung and determined effort to do so. One of the most populous nations on earth has made it a national aim to get rid of God, destroy the Bible, abolish the church, and undermine the foundations of Christian civilizations. This nation has as its teacher Nietzsche, who admonished his comrades thus: "I conjure you, my brethren, remain true to the earth and do not believe those who speak to you of supernatural hopes. They are poisoners, whether they know it or not. They are despoilers of life, decoying ones, and poisoned ones themselves, of whom the earth is weary; let them be gone."

Those who refuse to look up because they deny that there is any *One* to whom they may look, who have a spite against heaven because of the help it affords those who look up, who tell us that religion is the opiate of the people, are a great deal like the man about whom Carlyle wrote. He tells of a man who had a grudge against the stars and decided that he would blot them out. So he procured a huge squirtgun and filled it with muddy water and vigorously set about to accomplish his purpose. But the deluded soul succeeded in doing nothing more than bespatter himself and his friends with falling filthy water. The stars were still there. And so is God, in spite of disbelievers.

"The fool hath said in his heart, There is no God." When this declaration of disbelief is punctuated thus, it only illustrates what is so frequently true: that the real secret of infidelity is in the heart and not in the head, as so many would have us believe. Could we lay bare blatant disbelief and defiant infidelity, we would discover that much of it does not have its source in intellectual confusion nor honest doubt, but in lives that have strayed from the path of personal purity. Many who deny the existence of God are merely confessing, announcing to the world that they have strayed from the path of moral rectitude. They want to get rid of God so they can sin without remorse of conscience or fear of retribution. Someday, perhaps, these poor simpletons will discover the folly of their self-delusion, and then, like Adam and Eve, they will want to run and hide their naked souls from the judgment of God. Disbelieve if you will, but you cannot get rid of God so easily as all that. You may be able to avoid him here, but you cannot avoid him hereafter. How much better and wiser it is, then, to look up to him while he is still on the mercy seat, than it is to wait until you will have to look up to him on the judgment seat!

II

In the second place, the early morning uplook affords a helpful inlook. We get a glimpse of the status of our sinful selves as we behold the holiness of God and the sinlessness of his Son. The helpful effect of the morning uplook is well illustrated by the experience of Isaiah who, on going into the Temple with a burdened heart, and seeing the Lord high and lifted up, sitting upon a throne, exclaimed, "Woe is me! for I am undone; because I am a man of unclean lips, . . . for mine eyes have seen the King, the Lord of hosts." As he looked up to God he became painfully aware of the fact that he was a sinner. That is one of the blessed ministries of the morning uplook.

The helpful inlook that comes from the morning uplook begets in us a dissatisfaction with ourselves as we are. If one continues to look down, or about him on his own level, he is not likely to find any fault with himself. Rather, he is likely to take comfort in the fact that he compares favorably with others. But "they that measure themselves by themselves, and compare themselves among themselves, are not wise." There is only one with whom we should compare or measure ourselves, even Christ our Lord. And the moment we begin to look unto him, who though tempted in all points like as we are, yet without sin, there comes over us a deep sense of self-dissatisfaction. But it often takes something unusual to bring us to our senses, stir us out of our smug complacency and make us want to become better men and women. With Isaiah it was the death of Uzziah, the king in whom he and his nation had trusted for more than forty years. When God removed the temporal king, Isaiah saw the King eternal, high and lifted up; and there came into his life a divine discontent. As a result his lips were purged with a live coal from off the altar of God, and he offered himself, a servant of the King of kings.

It comes to this, then, that one of the principal ministries of the morning uplook is that it emancipates the worshiper from a haunting, hindering past. The remorse of memory is a terrible, tireless pursuer. "My sin is ever before me," was the lament of one who could not forget. In Hawthorne's *The Scarlet Letter* we see how terrible a haunting past may become. For seven long years Arthur Dimmesdale secretly suppresses a guilty conscience. But the day comes when he can no longer endure the remorse of memory. He mounts the pillory in the market place and takes his stand by the side of Hester, the girl he had wronged, and there before his townsmen he cries out: "Stands anyone here who questions God's judgment on a sinner? Behold, behold a dreadful witness of it." And laying open his shirt, baring his breast, he discloses the letter "A" that marks him the sinner he really was. He makes his confession that he might get rid of the pangs of a guilty conscience. Sidney Lanier has expressed what so many of us feel:

> My soul is sailing through the sea,
> But the past is heavy and hinders me;
> The past hath crusted cumbrous shells
> That hold the flesh of cold seamells
> About my soul.

> Old past, let go and drop in the sea,
> 'Till fathomless waters cover thee!
> For I am living, but thou art dead,
> Thou drawest back, I strive ahead.[1]

But how are we to be emancipated from a haunting, hindering past? We know that there is a downward drag in the very nature of man. Paul expressed it when he said: "For the good that I would I do not: but

---

[1]By permission of Charles Scribner's Sons, New York.

the evil which I would not, that I do. . . . When I
would do good, evil is present with me." Then, as if
in despair, he cries out, "O wretched man that I am!
who shall deliver me from the body of this death?"
But at last, with a shout of exultation, he answers his
own question, "Thanks be to God, which giveth us the
victory through our Lord Jesus Christ." In Jesus
Christ, then, we have an emancipator, one who can
deliver us from a sinful past. To him, and to him
alone, we must look and live.

> Look and live, my brother live,
> Look to Jesus now and live;
> 'Tis recorded in His word, Hallelujah!
> It is only that you look and live.

III

In the third place, the morning uplook provides a
wholesome outlook. We get a better perspective of
life. Indeed, one of the revelations of the uplook is
that it enables us to see what we by heaven's help may
yet become. Man can never become all that he is
capable of becoming without help from above. The
soul needs the help of heaven just as the flowers need
the sun and showers. They are rooted in the earth;
but the earth alone could never make them bloom in
all their beauty. They must have the uppull of heaven
as well as the uppush of mother earth. Even so it is
with the soul of man. For the present his feet are on
the earth; but the earth alone cannot bring him to
his full stature. He needs the uplift which heaven
alone can give. Such help is available in the morning
uplook. For one of the rewards of the morning uplook is that "heaven comes down our soul to greet,"

enabling us to "rise on stepping stones of our dead selves to higher things." "But they that wait upon the Lord shall renew their strength; they shall mount up with wings as eagles; they shall run, and not be weary; and they shall walk, and not faint."

One cannot practice the morning uplook and spend the day on a low moral level. The morning uplook, then, is more than a door of hope through which we get a glimpse of what we by the help of heaven may yet become. It has a distinctive ministry in that it furnishes the very means by which we rise from what we are to what we, through the grace of God, may yet become. It is a sort of Jacob's ladder on which we climb from our sinful selves to sons of God and joint heirs with Jesus Christ.

Furthermore, the morning uplook provides an ampler outlook. It enables us to push back the low-hanging horizon of life and make for ourselves a large place in which to dwell. As Abraham of old sat in his tent brooding over his circumscribed existence, the Lord "brought him forth abroad, and said, Look now toward heaven." And when he had obeyed, he found himself in a large place with life's horizon pushed back, and all worries about a cramped tent existence gone. The blessing of the wider outlook came to him through the ministry of the uplook. And when we begin to grow despondent over our cramped existence, we need to hear the voice of the Lord saying unto us, "Look now toward heaven." When the uplook has done its perfect work in us, we shall have an ampler outlook; life will be framed in a much wider margin.

IV

In the fourth place, since man must look up if he is to be lifted up from what he is to what he may become, ample provision for this exercise of the soul should be provided. And this God has done. He has so ordained the universe that all the natural light that illumines man's pathway comes from above. To him who has eyes to see, "The heavens declare the glory of God; and the firmament sheweth his handywork. Day unto day uttereth speech, and night unto night sheweth knowledge." Therefore, when we consider the heavens, the work of his hands, the moon and the stars which he has ordained, we are moved to exclaim, "O Lord, our Lord, how excellent is thy name in all the earth! who has set thy glory above the heavens." And just as all natural light comes from above, bidding man look up, even so "the true Light, which lighteth every man that cometh into the world," came from above, bidding man look up and live.

Besides, God ordained that one day in seven should be distinctly dedicated to the uplook exercises of the soul. The ministry of the Lord's day is to lift our eyes unto him who is the subject of our salvation, the object of our adoration, and the predicate of our faith, hope, and love. During the week our eyes, for the most part, are fixed on the things of this earth. But Sunday is God's call to us to come forth and look up, not down nor around. And he who heeds God's call and comes forth from the demoralizing effects of his week-day existence and seeks the help which heaven has to give, "shall be like a tree planted by the rivers of water, that bringeth forth his fruit in his season;

his leaf also shall not wither; and whatsoever he doeth shall prosper." But he who shuts himself away from God deprives himself of the help that heaven has to give, and denies himself the opportunities which Sunday provides for the uplook exercise of the soul, shall soon be destitute of any spiritual outlook.

The hours of worship on the Lord's Day is God's call to us to come forth from the cares of the world and exercise the soul in the art of the morning uplook. "We have to work to make a living. We have to worship to make a life." While at worship God bids us look unto him who is the author and the finisher of our faith, and not round about upon fellow worshipers as did the Pharisee, saying, "God, I thank thee that I am not as other men."

One of the best blessings that come from the morning uplook is that it lifts us above the faultfinding onlook,—the habit of looking about us with a critical eye,—and enables us to point the accusing finger at ourselves saying, "God be merciful unto me a sinner." If, while at worship, we will direct our prayer toward God instead of directing our criticism toward others, we will go down from the sanctuary with radiant faces, with hearts aglow, and with hands made ready for whatever work our Lord has for us to do.

Moreover, God has made provision for the exercise of the uplook in the unlifted Christ: "And I, if I be lifted up from the earth, will draw all men unto me."

> I saw One hanging on the tree,
>   In agony and blood;
> He fixed His languid eyes on me,
>   As near His cross I stood.

> It was for me, upon a tree
>   He died in agony,
> And now I give my life to live
>   For Him who died for me.

Yes, God hath highly exalted him and set him on high, even at his right hand, and given him a name that is above every other name, that at the mention of his name, every knee should bow and every tongue should confess that he is King of kings, and Lord of lords.   Therefore, look unto him and be ye lifted up, and be ye saved all the ends of the earth.

We return again to say, Here is the right way in which to begin the day: when you wake up, look up: "My voice shalt thou hear in the morning, O Lord; in the morning I will direct my prayer unto thee and will look up."

> I met God in the morning
>   When my day was at its best,
> And His presence came like sunrise,
>   Like a glory in my breast.
>
> All day long the Presence lingered,
>   All day long He stayed with me;
> And we sailed in perfect calmness
>   O'er a very troubled sea.
>
> Other ships were blown and battered,
>   Other ships were sore distressed.
> But the winds that seemed to drive them
>   Brought to us a peace and rest.
>
> So I think I know the secret,
>   Learned from many a troubled way:
> You must seek Him in the morning
>   If you want Him through the day[2]

---

[2] By permission of Bishop Ralph Spaulding Cushman, the author.

"FIFTH COLUMN" CHRISTIANS

Ye hypocrites, well did Esaias prophesy of you, saying, This people draweth nigh unto me with their mouth, and honoureth me with their lips; but their heart is far from me.—MATTHEW 15:7-8.

I

In recent days one of the oft-repeated tragedies in national defense in many lands has been the treachery and betrayal on the part of aliens who had been granted hospitality and permitted to enjoy the blessings and benefits of the country under whose flag they had selected to reside. More dastardly and despicable has been the deed when perpetrated by native sons who were regarded as loyal citizens and trusted as such. But whether aliens or disloyal citizens, upon them has fallen the odious name, "fifth column."

What name could more fittingly characterize the multitude of professed followers of Christ who share all the blessings and benefits of church membership, but shirk their duty, shun their responsibility, and assume an attitude of utter indifference to the claims of Christ upon their lives. There are thousands of members who show no more concern for the church and manifest no more interest in the cause of Christ than the vilest sinner about the street. A recent survey conducted by the "Committee on Local Church Emphasis" revealed the appalling facts that 47 per cent of the names on the rolls of the churches of our denomination are "names only"; and that 54 per cent do not attend public worship, serve, give, nor live as Christians should. All these are to Christianity and the church what the "fifth column" was to Norway, Denmark, Holland, Belgium, and France. They have enlisted in the army of the Lord, but have deserted his cause and are fraternizing and conniving with the enemy. Well did Christ characterize them when he said, "This people draweth nigh unto me with their mouth, and honoreth me with their lips; but their heart is far from me." They are the direct descendants of Judas, who drew near the Lord with his mouth,—kissed him, but alas! it was the kiss of Christianity's first "fifth columnist."

However, for this deplorable situation the church itself is partly to blame. Often there has been more anxiety about the quantity than the quality of the names added to the church. Too often pastors have been driven to the practice of member getting, because the "go-getter" minister has "stolen the show," has become more popular and in greater demand. Thus, it has been made entirely too easy to join the church, with the result that the names of many persons have been placed on the rolls without any evidence that there had been a genuine Christian experience. And, to our dismay, we are beginning to learn that an unregenerate membership very shortly becomes nothing more than a degenerate membership. Small wonder, then, that the church is not moving on with greater success! The whole Kingdom program is being sabotaged by the church's "fifth column."

The church should see to it that no one is permitted to remain in "good and regular standing" who is not willing to maintain a high average of Christian conduct, accept the responsibilities of church membership, and manifest an unqualified loyalty to the Captain of our salvation. Either by winning them to full allegiance to the Lord or by striking their names from the list of believers, the church must rid itself of its "fifth column." The sheep must be separated from the goats. It was for this sort of differentiation that the Apostle Paul was pleading when in his letter to the Corinthians he said, "Wherefore come out from among them, and be ye separate, saith the Lord."

But in complying with such an injunction we are confronted with certain difficulties, the first of which is ourselves. Not one of us can claim to be genuinely Christian in conduct and character. There are many impulses and inclinations in every one of us which are sufficient to hurry us on to moral ruin unless we practice a sturdy and a strict form of self-discipline. Paul voiced the reality of this truth when he declared: "For the good that I would I do not: but the evil which I would not, that I do. . . . O wretched man that I am! who shall deliver me from the body of this death?" In every one of us, in miniature at least, there is the making of a Dr. Jekyll and a Mr. Hyde.

> Within my earthly temple there's a crowd:
> There's one of us that's humble, one that's proud;
> There's one that's broken-hearted for his sins,
> And one that unrepentant sits and grins;
> There's one that loves his neighbor as himself,
> And one that cares for naught but fame and pelf.
> From much perplexing care I would be free
> If I could once determine which is Me![1]
>
> —ANON.

Moreover, we are compelled to keep company with and to live in close proximity to persons who have deserted Christ's cause and have digressed from the path of moral rectitude. Against the subtle and sinister influence which these "fifth column" Christians have over us we have to battle daily. Constantly, either by word or by example, they plead, "Come thou with us"; and lacking the moral stamina to resist, not a few yield, desert Christ, and join the ranks of the enemy.

Besides all this, the subtle form of propaganda used by fifth columnists makes it hard for some to remain steadfast in their allegiance. A method practiced in high places as well as low, in the classroom as well as in the market place, is sneering at and making fun of faith and Christian standards of conduct. This was the method employed by those who prepared Christ for his crucifixion. They took off his own clothes and dressed him up in the mock robes of royalty and made fun of him. But their jibes and taunts availed them nothing. He refused to be stampeded into digressing from the purpose for which he came into the world. And you need not be stampeded into denying your Lord and turning traitor to his cause just because some fifth columnists make fun of your faith or sneer at your religion. Have some convictions of your own,— convictions for which you are willing to die if need be. Possess for yourself

> A faith that will not shrink
>   Though pressed by every foe,
> That will not tremble on the brink
>   Of any earthly woe.

II

Lamentable indeed is the fact that the life of so many professed followers of Christ betrays the faith which their lips profess. "Well did Esaias prophesy of you, saying, This people draweth nigh unto me with their mouth, and honoureth me with their lips; but their heart is far from me." As a result, the chief peril of the church today is not from without, but from within. This, in large measure, accounts for the fact that Christianity is not influencing the life of the world as it did in apostolic days. The early disciples, though few in number, made such a profound impression on the social, political, moral, and religious life of their day that they were accused of turning the world upside down. And the secret of their influence was due to the fact that theirs was no mere lip loyalty. They dared to die rather than renounce their allegiance to their Lord. But because present-day Christians lack the courage, the self-denial, the sacrificial spirit possessed by the early heroes of faith, Christianity has had a serious setback in recent years. Today it is on the defensive in many lands.

The record of Christian history furnishes abundant proof that the sort of Christians who have impressed the world and won respect were men and women who dared to obey God rather than man, who did what the Lord said as well as what he did. It always has been and still is essential that Christians be able to "tell what great things the Lord has done" for them; but more important still is that they give a demonstration of what he has done by doing what he said. We might gather here in this sanctuary Sunday after Sunday and have as our theme song,

> All hail the power of Jesus' name!
> Let angels prostrate fall;
> Bring forth the royal diadem,
> And crown him Lord of all!

and do nothing more than draw nigh unto him with our mouth and honor him with our lips. Unless we rise up and go forth and do his will, obey his word, and walk in his way, the world will call us hypocrites and look upon us with contemptuous scorn, and rightly so.

The day has come when we who profess faith in God the Father and in Jesus Christ his only begotten Son must quit saying to every half-baked agnostic and to every embryonic atheist: "Yes, there is a great deal of truth in what you say about the Bible. Much of it is myth and folklore." We must hear and heed the exhortation of Mary the mother of Jesus who admonished the servants at the wedding feast saying, "Whatever he tells you to do, do it." To put it plainly, the sort of Christians needed just now are those who believe that Jesus spoke with divine authority, and are willing to do what he said.

In recent years we have heard a great deal about doubt and unbelief and the danger of paganism and atheism. But more dangerous to the success of Christianity is the avowed or implied conviction on the part of many professed followers of Christ that much of what he said need not be taken seriously. Instead of regarding him as one who knew what he was talking about and meant what he said, there are altogether too many who take literally such sayings as fit their selfish standards of conduct and reject other sayings which run counter to their worldly ways. They may not publicly deny nor openly reject any particular saying of Jesus; but what is worse, they profess to believe what he said and then live as though he had not said it. Is there any wonder that we raise the alarm over the presence of "fifth column" Christians in the churches today?

Of the many soul-searching sayings of Jesus, none has a sharper edge than this, "This people draweth nigh unto me with their mouth, and honoureth me with their lips; but their heart is far from me." These words have a stab and a sting which are unsurpassed by anything else he said. In them he is confronting doubtful disciples with the sin of saying what they do not mean, of lip loyalty and life apostasy.

We profess to believe that Christ is the Son of God and that he speaks with divine authority; but we often live as though his words carry no more weight than if they had been spoken by a mere man. Many of us are like Mr. Massingham, late editor of the *London Nation,* who said, "I am fond of Jesus Christ, but I never make an effort to do what he tells me to do." Yes, we draw nigh unto him with the mouth and honor him with the lips and let it go at that. All too often, instead of undertaking to make our ways comply with his word, we endeavor to make his word conform to our ways. When confronted with some hard and difficult saying of his we deftly dodge it or cleverly explain it away. We have become expert exegetes in the art of interpreting his teachings in keeping with our selfish standards of living.

But let us not forget that when God said, "This is my beloved Son, . . . hear ye him," he was warning us against dodging the plain and obvious meaning of Christ's words or denaturing them by clever exegesis. He was admonishing us to accept the words of his beloved Son without hesitation, without mental reservation or secret evasion of mind. And when his words cut right straight across our wilful ways or run counter to our cherished plans, we hear Jesus say, "Why call ye me, Lord, Lord, and do not the things which I say?"

III

The tragedy of Christianity today is that multitudes who profess to be the redeemed children of God are not in conduct and character distinguishable from the sons of Satan. Christians should stand out separate and distinct from the world,—in the world, but not a part of nor a party to its wrongdoing. "Holy Father," said Jesus, "I pray not that thou shouldest take them out of the world, but that thou shouldest keep them from the evil."

Jesus was forever telling his followers that they must be men whose conduct and character marked them as different. "Come out from among them, and be ye separate, saith the Lord." Ye shall be like "a city that is set on a hill"; like a candle that is set on a stand, "and giveth light unto all that are in the house"; "Ye are the light of the world. . . . Let your light so shine before men, that they may see your good works, and glorify your Father which is in heaven." But in a sinful world, a world in which more than 50 per cent of all who profess faith in Christ are "fifth col-

umn" Christians, it takes moral courage to stand out
"like a city that is set on a hill," like a candle aflame
in a conspicuous place in the dark. He who dares to
do so must have some strong convictions, convictions
sturdy enough to enable him to stand up and take the
consequences.

All too many Christians cleverly play the part of a
chameleon by assuming the color and character of every
situation in which they find themselves. When placed
against a religious background they take on the appear-
ance of saints; but when placed against the sordid
background of the world they take on the characteristics
of sinners. This was the part that Peter tried to play
as he entered the outer court of the judgment hall of
Pilate and warmed himself at the fire kindled by the
enemies of Christ. To hide his identity he undertook
to assume the characteristics of the company in which
he found himself. He became a ruffian: he cursed and
swore.

But we had better not be in a hurry to condemn Peter,
for we often show ourselves very like him: wicked
worldlings when placed among the enemies of Christ.
When invited to a social function which is in conflict
with Christian standards of conduct, instead of declin-
ing we usually say, "I shall be delighted to accept your
gracious invitation." And once at the party we par-
take of whatever is provided, whether it is merely
spiked or unadulterated. What is your attitude when
you find yourself at some social function which calls
for conformity to conduct unbecoming to a Christian?
Do you acquiesce, indulge, identify yourself with the
company in which you find yourself? Do you warm

yourself at the fire kindled by fifth columnists, or do you politely but very positively decline? In such an hour you should remember the admonition of the Apostle Paul, "Be not conformed to this world."

What do you suppose would happen if the more than fifty million Christians in America were loyal citizens of the kingdom of God and were honestly and enthusiastically working to establish Christ's way of life? This, I think, would happen: the pagan practices which go on in our social, economic, and political life would be altered forthwith. The world is not waiting for more eloquent preaching of the gospel of Christ, but for more eloquent practicing on the part of his professed followers. The cause of Christ is not suffering for want of recruits, but from apostasy on the part of multitudes who profess faith in his name. We often raise an alarm over the harm that atheism is doing, and I am not ignorant of the fact that it is busy in many of our colleges and universities subtly undermining the faith of young people; but Christianity has a greater enemy within its own ranks: "fifth columnists." If Christianity ever suffers defeat it will be because it has been betrayed by the indifferent and the disloyal citizens within its own kingdom.

The loss of the prestige of the church is due primarily to the failure of her adherents to obey the injunction, "Come out from among them, and be ye separate, saith the Lord." Because of this fact, the church has well-nigh lost its right of protest; at least its protest has become ineffective. If the church is ever able to make its protest effective, then the men and the women who make up "the body of Christ" must give a satisfactory answer to Christ's question, "Why call ye me, Lord, Lord, and do not the things which I say?"

IV

To be sure, objections arise in the minds of men when a minister stresses and presses home the sharp points of a text like this. One of the first protests raised is that we cannot deal with the apostasy of church members as we do with the disloyalty of members of a fraternity, a lodge, or a civic club. We are reminded that Christ said that the tares and the wheat must grow together until the harvest. Maybe so! but there should be no mistaking the tares for the wheat nor the wheat for the tares. The one should be easily distinguishable from the other. But, alas! too often they are so much alike that the one is mistaken for the other.

Another objection that leaps to the lips and makes protest against the plea that Christians take their religion seriously and honestly undertake to do what Christ says, is that we would get ourselves rated as fools and fanatics. But need I remind you that this was just the kind of courage possessed by the early Christians: "We are counted fools for Christ's sake," said the Apostle Paul.

To be sure, we are not pleading for an eccentric nor for a fanatical brand of Christianity. Already we have too much of that type springing up here and there. No, I am not urging any foolhardy following of Christ, but a sane and wholehearted acceptance of his way of life. However, of one thing we may be sure: there is no need of admonishing ourselves to beware of taking Jesus' words so seriously and doing them so literally that we shall be accused of being eccentrics or fanatics. I see no evidence whatever that Christians are in any danger of throwing caution to the winds in an effort to do Christ's will and take his way of life. Our real danger is in being so cautious, so calculating, so practical, and so scientific that we shall secretly condemn Jesus as an impractical idealist and lay aside his gospel as something "too high and good for human nature's daily food."

Certainly these distressful days demand that Christians be Christlike in character and conduct. Why defend Christ's deity if we will not accept and exalt his lordship over our lives? "Why call ye me, Lord, Lord, and do not the things which I say?" Of what value are we to the cause of Christ if on Monday our lives betray the faith which our lips profess on Sunday? The world is judging Christianity by your conduct and mine. We are Christ's epistles, read and known of all men.

We know that Christ has a secret to impart: peace for our troubled hearts: and for a war torn world: "My peace I give unto you." But we are reluctant to accept the terms on which he promises to impart his peace. We know that in him we may secure power for victorious living; but we are inclined to trust in our own strength and lean to our own understanding with the result that we are baffled, bewildered, and impotent. One thing is becoming increasingly evident: if civilization is to be saved from utter destruction at the hands of warmongers and men gone mad with lust for power, then this old world must be taught and brought to accept Christ's way of life. This was the mission the

Master committed to his followers. And if the millions who profess faith in his name would "heed what he saith, do what he willeth," the present world calamity could be coined into capital for Christ and this old war torn world turned back to God.

Today, when Christianity is on the defensive and paganism grows apace in many lands, is no time for Christians to be guilty of heartlessly and hypocritically drawing nigh unto Christ with their mouth and honoring him with their lips. The day demands that Christians shall dare to stand up and speak up for Jesus.

> Stand up, stand up for Jesus!
>   Ye soldiers of the cross;
> Lift high His royal banner,
>   It must not suffer loss:
> From vict'ry unto vict'ry
>   His army shall he lead,
> Till ev'ry foe is vanquished.
>   And Christ is Lord indeed.
>
> Stand up, stand up for Jesus!
>   The trumpet call obey;
> Forth to the mighty conflict,
>   In this His glorious day:
> Ye that are men, now serve Him,
>   Against unnumbered foes;
> Let courage rise with danger,
>   And strength to strength oppose.
>
> Stand up, stand up for Jesus!
>   Stand in His strength alone;
> The arm of flesh will fail you;
>   Ye dare not trust your own:
> Put on the gospel armor,
> Each piece put on with prayer;
> Where duty calls, or danger,
>   Be never wanting there.

VI

HAMANISM

So they hanged Haman on the gallows that he had prepared for
Mordecai.—ESTHER 7:10.

I

For some unknown reason fortune had highly favored Haman. One regal honor after another had
been conferred on him. He had been promoted until
he was little less than both conscience and will to the
king. He had become the power behind the throne.
He had only to speak, and it was done by royal decree.

Once he had cleverly wormed his way into a place
of great influence, he subtly sought to make himself
indispensable at the king's court. He was a past-
master in the art of flattery; and almost clairvoyant
in his ability to discern the king's moods and attitudes.
If he had been cast in a nobler mold, and had pursued
a more honorable course, he might have been to Ahasuerus what Joseph was to Pharaoh. But he lacked the
quality of character Joseph possessed. Promotion, position, and honor did for him just what they so often do
for men of his measure: spoiled him hopelessly. He
proved to be a little man in a large place. He was ob-
sessed with a racial prejudice that was nothing short
of madness. And the tragedy of it was that he had
only to commit his hatred to writing, decreeing the
annihilation of the people he hated, and it became the
law of the realm over the signature of the king.

In due time it came to pass that a Hebrew by the
name of Mordecai failed to salute him in due and an-

cient form: "Mordecai bowed not, nor did him reverence." And Haman went red with rage. His vanity filled him with vicious madness toward anyone who failed to bow to his vaunted greatness. Forthwith he proceeded to plot the destruction of the offender and "all the Jews that were throughout the whole kingdom of Ahasuerus, even the people of Mordecai." Said he to the king: "There is a certain people scattered abroad and dispersed among the people in all the provinces of thy kingdom; and their laws are diverse from all people; neither keep they the king's laws: therefore it is not for the king's profit to suffer them. If it please the king, let it be written that they be destroyed: and I will pay ten thousand talents of silver to the hands of those that have the charge of the business."

To this satanic scheme the king gave his assent. He took off his signet ring and gave it to Haman saying, "The silver is given to thee, the people also, to do with them as it seemeth good to thee." What more did Haman the Jew hater want? He wasted no time in calling the king's scribe, to whom he dictated letters and sealed them with the king's signet ring and sent them by post into all the provinces. The letters gave orders "to destroy, to kill, and to cause to perish, all Jews, both young and old, little children and women, in one day." Thus, Haman's hate was to fall as a blitzkrieg upon the Jews. They were to be annihilated "in one day." A rather ambitious undertaking, and for no better reason than to gratify Haman's hatred for one Jew in particular, and for all Jews in general! Nothing less than selfish madness could drive a man to such ends of revenge.

The news of Haman's sinister plot came to the attention of Mordecai, the particular Jew against whom Haman had a growing grudge. He sent word to Esther, the queen, his cousin whom he had reared, imploring her to intercede with the king in behalf of her people. She replied, "Whosoever, whether man or woman, shall come unto the king into the inner court, who is not called, there is one law of his to put him to death, except such to whom the king shall hold out the golden sceptre." But Mordecai reminded the queen that she, being a Jewess, would not escape, and added the telling prophecy, "Who knoweth whether thou art come to the kingdom for such a time as this?" When Esther received this message she sent word to Mordecai saying, "And so will I go in unto the king, . . . and if I perish, I perish." And true to her promise, taking her life in her hand, she went in before the king. But happily he held out the golden scepter and inquired, "What is thy request? it shall be even given thee to the half of the kingdom." For the present, Esther's only petition was that the king and Haman come to a banquet which she that day had prepared. This pleased the king, and he sent word to Haman to make haste and do as Esther had requested. Once they were at the banquet, the king turned to Esther and said, "What is thy petition? and it shall be granted thee: and what is thy request? even to the half of the kingdom it shall be performed." Again, the queen's request was similar to the first. Said she, "If I have found favour in the sight of the king, and if it please the king to grant my petition, and to perform my request, let the king and Haman come to the banquet that I shall prepare for them, and I will do to morrow as the king hath said."

"Then went Haman forth that day joyful and with a glad heart." On arriving at his home, "he sent . . . for his friends, and Zeresh his wife," and boastingly related to them how the king had honored and advanced him above all the princes. "Yea," said he, "the queen did let no man come in with the king unto the banquet that she had prepared but myself; and to morrow am I invited unto her also with the king" to another banquet. "Yet," said he sullenly, "all this availeth me nothing, so long as I see Mordecai the Jew sitting at the king's gate." Whereupon adoring Mrs. Haman made a helpful suggestion, and all his friends chimed their approval. Like infamous Jezebel, or despicable Lady Macbeth, she admonished her husband to murder the man who stood in his way. Said she, "Let a gallows be made of fifty cubits high, and to morrow speak thou unto the king that Mordecai may be hanged thereon: then go thou in merrily with the king unto the banquet." Just as if a man could have a merry heart and a good appetite with a murdered man on his conscience! But if ever there was a man who could, he was Haman. Therefore, it is written, "And the thing pleased Haman; and he caused the gallows to be made."

II

Thus far Haman has been working his will and having his way unhindered and uninterrupted. But at last he has come to a juncture where he is to be confronted with formidable opposition from a Power with which he had not hitherto reckoned. Very shortly Mordecai would have dangled from the gallows that Haman had prepared for him if the hand of God had not intervened. But the very night of the would-be-hanging, the Spirit of God disturbed the king so that he could not sleep. At the promptings of none other than Providence, he requested that "the book of records of the chronicles" be brought in and read to him. As the scribe began to read, it was not by accident that the following passage fell with a thud on the ears of the king: "And it was found written, that Mordecai had told of Bigthana and Teresh, two of the king's chamberlains, the keepers of the door, who sought to lay hand on the king." In other words, this passage reminded the king that Mordecai had saved him from being murdered by two of his trusted doorkeepers. When the king heard the reminder he asked, "What honour and dignity hath been done to Mordecai for this?" And he was told, "There is nothing done for him."

At this juncture, just as if his presence had been providentially timed, Haman appeared in the outer court. He had come to speak to the king about hanging Mordecai on the gallows that he had made ready in his own back yard. But God had decreed that Haman should perform quite another mission. For no one can read the sequel to Haman's murderous designs on Mordecai without seeing the hand of God thrust forth to turn abruptly the course of events. Therefore, when Haman came in before the king, he had on his mind one thing and the king had in mind quite another. The king was the first to speak. Said he, "What shall be done unto the man whom the king delighteth to honour?"

The conceited, self-centered Haman said to himself, The king can have in mind no one but myself.
And he answered accordingly. Now was his chance,
thought he, to let the people know what the king
thought of Haman. So he proposed that the man whom
the king delighteth to honor be paraded through the
streets in royal apparel, on the king's horse, with the
royal crown on his head, and with a footman to run
before proclaiming: "Thus shall it be done to the man
whom the king delighteth to honour." Then to Haman's horror the king commanded, "Make haste, and
take the apparel and the horse, as thou hast said, and
do even so to Mordecai the Jew, that sitteth at the
king's gate: let nothing fail of all that thou hast
spoken."

With a heavy heart Haman did as he was bidden,
and then went home to break the sad news to Mrs.
Haman. While he was yet speaking, the king's cham-
berlain came to bring him to the second banquet which
the queen had prepared for him and the king. At the
banquet table the king again inquired, "What is thy
petition, queen Esther? and it shall be granted thee:
and what is thy request? and it shall be performed,
even to the half of the kingdom." Like a bolt out of
the blue her answer fell on the ears of Haman: "If I
have found favour in thy sight, O king, and if it
please the king, let my life be given me at my petition, and my people at my request: for we are sold, I
and my people, to be destroyed, to be slain, and to perish." "Who is he," asked the king, "and where is he,
that durst presume in his heart to do so?" Alas! had
he so soon forgotten? At last Esther was master of

the situation. She pointed the finger of accusation at Haman and said, "The adversary and enemy is this wicked Haman."

The king was so deeply shaken by this unexpected revelation that he got up from the banquet table and went out into the garden. When he returned he found "Haman was fallen upon the bed whereon Esther was." Mistaking his posture as a mortal insult to the queen, he angrily exclaimed, "Will he force the queen also before me in the house?" Harbonah, one of the palace chamberlains, overheard the threatening words of the king and came forward with the timely suggestion, "Behold also, the gallows fifty cubits high, which Haman had made [in his own house] for Mordecai, who had spoken good for the king." And to his subtle suggestion the king promptly replied, "Hang him thereon. So they hanged Haman on the gallows that he had prepared for Mordecai."

III

In Haman we find a big hunk of human nature, the counterpart of ourselves. In every one of us there is tendency closely akin to the spirit manifested in this man of ancient history. For who of us, at sometime or other, in the evil imaginations of the mind, has not secretly builded a gallows on which to hang the one he hated? When some Mordecai gets in our way, or fails to manifest the respect which we fancy we deserve, or endangers the position which we occupy, or threatens to take away the honor which we covet, we are prone to deal with him in true Hamanistic fashion.

Human nature is very much the same today as it was in that bygone day. Hamanism was not hanged with Haman; it still persists. But the story of Haman should be a striking and a startling reminder of the disaster toward which racial prejudice and malicious dislike drive with deadly determination, perfect precision, and exact accuracy. They dethrone reason, unbalance judgment, destroy justice, and whip up a fury that finally oversteps all bounds of propriety.

If only we had a free hand, we might have revenge to our full satisfaction, without any fear of retribution. But this old story teaches us that "There is a divinity that shapes our ends"; One who has ordained that "Whatsoever a man soweth, that shall he also reap"; One who bringeth our wicked devices to naught. Maddened by hate and crazed by racial prejudice, Haman set about to destroy all Jews and to hang the particular Jew against whom he had a personal grudge. But alas! Haman was hanged on the gallows that he prepared for Mordecai.

Therefore, when in the name of patriotism some modern Haman sets about to pillage and destroy the race he hates, his pretended patriotism becomes hollow hypocrisy. Even those who hitherto delighted to honor him turn away in disgust and mete out to him the punishment he deserves. "So they hanged Haman on the gallows that he prepared for Mordecai." Knowing that God's moral law is inexorable, we may expect to witness some significant hangings within the near future.

Adolph Hitler is our most notorious modern example of Hamanism. His diabolical decrees against the Jews might well have been copied from the fiendish letters written by Haman. For, like Haman, he hates the Jews and is resolved to drink deep from the cup of sweet revenge. But let Hitler beware! for in the bottom of the cup he is very likely to find the dregs of hemlock instead of honey. Of the poisonous potion he has mixed for the Jews, he himself will one day drink. For one of the paradoxes of life is that the poisonous potion which one prepares for a foe, he himself is finally compelled to drink.

Both literature and life bear witness to this fact. In general, this is the theme of Shakespeare's *Macbeth,* particularly in the following lines,

> But in these cases
> We still have judgment here; that we but teach
> Bloody instruction, which, being taught, return
> To plague the inventor: this even-handed justice
> Commends the ingredients of our poison'd chalice
> To our own lips.

And to this same truth the psalmist bears testimony when he declares, "His mischief shall return upon his own head, and his violent dealing shall come down upon his own pate." Violence does, in truth, recoil upon the violent, and the schemer falls into the pit which he digs for another. In more graphic words, Dr. Moffatt translates the passage:

> The scoundrel is alive with malice,
>   hatching mischief and deception;
> he digs out a deep pit—
>   and into his own pitfall he shall tumble!
> His mischief shall recoil on his own head,
>   His violence shall drop on his own crown.
>   —Psalm 7:16-18.

This being true, we may expect that just as Haman dangled at the end of the noose which he prepared for Mordecai, even so Hitler will one day hang.

IV

The sad sequel to the story of Haman's hate should teach us the solemn lesson that the man who tries to get even never gets ahead. For the moral law is arrayed against the avenger, and sooner or later measures to him the justice he deserves. When we take the tragic sequel to the story of Haman's hate for the Jews as an illustration of the response the moral law makes to race prejudice, we find in it a solemn warning for ourselves. Retribution is only the natural response of the moral law to the spirit of revenge.

No one can go about harboring hate in his heart and storing up revenge in his mind and not have his whole life colored by the evil emotions that run riot through his soul. Hate harbored in the heart soon shows in the face.

There is a story in the Bible which illustrates this truth. Miriam, the sister of Moses, became jealous and envious of her distinguished brother. Like Haman, she set about to get him out of the way and take for herself the honor which belonged to him. But she was rewarded with the telltale evidence of leprosy in her face. But there was leprosy in her heart before the disease appeared in her face. If one cared to be personal, one might name some living examples—men and women on whose faces there is written the telltale evidence of long harbored hate.

Hate in the heart not only shows in the countenance, it crops out in conduct as well. The trouble with the person whose mind is poisoned with prejudice and inflamed with dislike is that he is unable to see the end toward which his malice is driving him. He nurses his grudge until it becomes big enough to master him. He succeeds in persuading himself that he is justified in preparing a gallows on which to hang the one for whom he harbors ill will. But Jesus expressed in words what so many experience in life: "With what measure you mete, it shall be measured to you again." Yet, many seem to think that they are clever enough to evade the moral law. They are confident that that which happened to Haman will not befall them. Therefore, they go on practicing Hamanism until they bring down upon their heads the fate that befell him.

One may start with a just cause, but, if in the spirit of revenge justice is pushed to the point of persecution, then the persecuted becomes a martyr and the persecutor loses the respect and support of those who were formerly friendly to his cause. But to start with an unjust cause, one founded on a fancied slight, or based on race prejudice, and in a spirit of malicious revenge push it to the point of persecution,—that is Hamanism and deserves Haman's reward.

Before setting about to build a gallows for the one you would like to destroy, you had better meditate on the hanging of Haman. Revenge becomes a deadly boomerang. When you work yourself into a frenzy by feeding dislike with sweet morsels of revenge, you had better beware! For one of the paradoxes of life is that the would-be executioner becomes the executed.

I made the cross myself, whose weight
   Was later laid on me.
This thought is torture as I toil
   Up life's steep Calvary.

To think my own hands drove the nails!
   I sang a merry song,
And chose the heaviest wood I had
   To build it firm and strong.

If I had guessed—if I had dreamed
   Its weight was meant for me,
I should have made a lighter cross
   To bear up Calvary[1]

---

[1]"A Little Parable," by Anne Reeve Aldrich. Used by permission of Charles Scribner's Sons, New York.

VII

SAID A SON TO HIS FATHER

A certain man had two sons: and the younger of them said to his father, Father, give me the portion of goods that falleth to me.— LUKE 15:11-12.

I

Here was a young man who was about to enter upon an independent career. But before he fared forth he came to require at the hands of his father equipment for the venture. That was his inalienable right. No father has a right to send his son into the battle of life without arming him with the very best equipment he can provide.

But, like this son of parable fame, many a young man makes the mistake of thinking that the chief equipment for life consists in the abundance of things one possesses. And for this false philosophy a father is often responsible. By the way he lives he gives the impression that money makes the man and want of it the fellow. He spends his days doing little else than accumulating as large a portion of this world's goods as he can get together to pass on to his children. But alas! that which he intends to be an advantage very often turns out to be a serious disadvantage. For history tends to prove that they who inherit much amount to little.

However, we need not be misled by the fact that this young man's request seemed to deal with material values alone. He had a right to much else besides, much that his father was able to bestow had he been in a receptive attitude. But the trouble with him was that he was not in the right mood to permit his father to deliver anything other than a due portion of this world's goods. It was not until he came to himself and returned in a different attitude that his father was able to confer on him his spiritual birthright.

Let us get this clearly in mind: When a son stands up to say, "Father, give me the portion of goods that falleth to me," he is not limited to stocks, bonds, big bank account, nor a flourishing business. He should be calling for a more praiseworthy patrimony than that,—a legacy of life more precious than gold, yea than much fine gold.

II

The first portion that justly falleth to a son is the right to be wellborn. To be required to start life within the shadow of a bad name is a handicap that is difficult to overcome. "A good name is rather to be chosen than great riches, and loving favor is better than silver or gold." Every father should see to it that his children are blessed with the advantage of being born to a name that is unsullied by sin. If potential parents could hear the request of the sons who are to be, I think they would hear them clamoring for the right to be wellborn. No man has a right to conduct his premarital life in such a way as to pass on tainted blood to his offspring. But that is just what all too many potential fathers are doing. As a result we may expect that little children will be born into the world blind and blighted in body and mind. A most pathetic example came under my observation. A young man, before marriage, broke the seventh commandment and as a result contracted a loathsome disease. He went to Dr. Cure'm Quick who, after a little superficial treatment, assured him that he was well again. A few weeks afterward he was married. In due time there was born to him a son who appeared to be normal until he approached the latter teens. Then it was that the sins of the father were visited upon the son. At first his eyes began to fail. Then he began to lose control of his muscular movements. Today he is a helpless, hopeless human wreck,—all because he was deprived of his right to be wellborn.

In the second place, a son has a right to the portion of being well-bred, the right to the best education a father can provide. No boy can grow to the full stature of his manhood without an education. The Bible declares that one cannot, by taking thought, add a single cubit to one's stature. But we have long since learned that one can increase his stature several cubits by taking thought—by the proper cultivation of the mind. Consider how an education increases the stature! The educated man, other things being equal, stands head and shoulders above the uneducated man. Someone has said that a person with a high school education has 87 times the chance over the non-high school graduate of performing distinguished service; and a college education gives a man 800 times the chance over the non-college graduate of performing distinguished service. In other words, a high school education increases one's stature about 87 per cent above that at which one stands without it; and a college education increases one's stature about 800 per cent above that at which one stands without it.

But more is involved in being well-bred than merely increasing one's earning capacity or chances to succeed. It has to do with culture, refinement of personality, and the improvement of the whole man. It is that something which gives virtue to conduct, color to disposition, and tone to one's attitude toward others.

In the third place, a son has a right to the portion of being well-led. He is not going to listen long to the advice of a father who does not practice what he preaches. Not every son will have the good sense to follow the example a father sets. Nevertheless, it is the duty of a father to present to his son the portion of goods that justly falleth to him by way of a good example. Let every father be apprized of this fact: a son is never well-led until he has been shown how to walk in the way with Christ. A father has not done his full duty until he can say, as said that father of old, "Master, I have brought unto thee my son."

Such a day as came to the father of parable fame comes to every father: a day on which a son stands up to require of him equipment for life. Woe be unto him who has squandered his substance, dissipated his powers, and comes to that day a moral and spiritual bankrupt, unable to deliver the portion of goods that rightly falleth to a son!

III

Said a father to a son, "Son, give me the portion of goods that falleth to me." If a son has a right to require of a father the portion of goods that falleth to him, certainly a father has a right to require something of a son. But the danger is that a son may think that father owes him everything and that he owes

father nothing. If a son has a right to the portion of
goods that falleth to him, a father has a right to in-
quire what he intends to do with it. That is a fair
question, one that not only a father has a right to ask,
but one that society too may justly ask.

There are three ways in which a son may make his
reply to this question. In the first place, he may play
the prodigal on a grand scale. Heedless of the past,
careless of the present, and indifferent to the future,
he may wilfully and wantonly waste his inheritance.
That is just what the son of parable fame did. He
gathered his all together, fared forth, and wasted his
substance in riotous living and was soon in want. And
there are all too many young men in our day who are
following his example. They call for their portion with
no other intention than to squander it in wanton ways.
The chief sin of not a few today is the sin of wast-
ing life's legacy, that free gift which has come to
them from their parents in particular and from the
past in general.

In the second place, like the one-talent man in Jesus'
parable, a son can lay life's legacy away in a napkin,
or dig a hole in the earth and bury it. The most despicable man in all the world is he who has received
much and has done nothing with it. According to
Harvey's grammar his gender is "neuter," neither male
nor female, just an "it," here to take up room, a mere
cumberer of the ground.

On an occasion I was dining with one of my dea-
cons. He had as his guest a man from a distant city.
During the course of the meal the conversation turned
to a discussion of a man's contribution to society. I

ventured the suggestion that a man's contribution should be commensurate with his privileges and opportunities; that the secret of success is in making the most of what one has; that the man to be admired is he who starts with little and achieves much; that the most despicable man is he who starts with much and amounts to nothing. I did not know at the time how near to being personal my remarks had been; for the visitor, with an expression of wistful sadness and longing, said: "My one regret is that I did not make better use of my life. I was a privileged son. Had I taken advantage of my privileges and improved my opportunities I might have made a worthy contribution to society. But it is too late now to begin." He was a man well on in his sixties. Later I learned that he had inherited wealth, but had done nothing to add to what he had received. He had simply lived on the interest of the wealth accumulated by another. In the judgment of the Master there is no man who deserves more severe condemnation than the man who fails to make use of that with which he has been entrusted.

In the third place, a son may turn his legacy loose and let it work for himself and for the welfare of others. Indeed that is the duty of all; but how much more so of him who has received much. "For unto whomsoever much is given, of him shall be much required." While one may squander his legacy or lay it aside and neglect it, he has no moral right to do so. We are the heirs of the ages. But we are more; we are trustees as well. We are in debt to the past, responsible for the present, and accountable for the future. Having received our portion, we are not only under

obligation to protect it, we are duty-bound to pass it
on to posterity with usury.

Great indeed is the portion that rightly falleth to
a son. He is the beneficiary of all the ages. It is all
his by right. But he has no right to waste it. To do
so is, in the language of one who made that mistake,
to sin against father, home, and heaven, and to reduce
one to the level of a hired servant instead of an heir.

Therefore, the question a son should seriously consider is, What shall I do with my paternal legacy?
How shall I dispose of it? To what market, if any,
shall I go that I may invest my patrimony for the
good of myself and the benefit of society? Here is
a responsibility no son can shun. He can do whatever
he will with his portion, and no man can hinder him.
But he cannot escape the consequences. He may carry
his all to the market of Vanity Fair and there exchange
what he has for the pleasures of earth and the satis-
factions of the flesh. But let him beware! for the
principal stall at that market place is the devil's booth:

> At the Devil's booth, all things are sold,
> Each ounce of dross costs its ounce of gold;
> For a cap and bells our lives we pay,
> Bubbles we buy with a whole soul's tasking.

But there is another market to which he may go, it
is the market of the Master. Here, in exchange for
the old life he may receive a life made new: "Therefore
if any man be in Christ, he is a new creature; old
things are passed away; behold, all things are become
new." Therefore, said a father to his son, "Son, claim
the portion that rightly belongs to you, gather your all

together and hie yourself to the market of the Master. Invest what you have with him and you shall have 'treasures in heaven, where neither moth nor rust doth corrupt, and where thieves do not break through nor steal.' "

VIII

THE BETTER SAMARITAN

And one of them, when he saw that he was healed, turned back, and with a loud voice glorified God, and fell down on his face at his feet, giving him thanks: and he was a Samaritan.—LUKE 17: 15-16.

I

Here were ten men who were outwardly alike, but inwardly different,—they were lepers. Since misery loves company, their misfortune had made them boon companions. Driven from society, they sought what little comfort they could find in the fellowship of one another.

These ten lepers heard of the miraculous cures of the Christ, and together went forth to find him. And when they came near him they prayed to him to have mercy on them and heal them. They not only prayed, they obeyed. For when, in reply to their pathetic petition, Jesus said, "Go shew yourselves unto the priests," they went without any question. Disappointed they may have been, but they were not disobedient. Doubtless they thought that he would lay his hands on them and heal them, or say unto them, "Be clean!" But instead he said, "Go shew yourselves unto the priests." This they were required to do after they were healed. It was the only way in which they could be reinstated in society. But while the leprosy was still upon them they were told to go and show themselves to the priests. It was not easy for them to obey. Why undertake to get an audience with the priests while the leprosy was still upon them? But it was not theirs to ask the reason why; it was theirs to do or die. Therefore, they proved their faith by their obedience, and Jesus justified their faith by healing them.

The ten men who appeared to be so much alike in the day of their distress proved to be quite different on the day of their deliverance from the dreadful disease. Nine of them went on their way forgetful of their bene-factor. Only one of them returned to give thanks to him who had healed them. The nine had received that for which they prayed, and considered the transaction closed. They felt no obligation to return and express their gratitude to the One from whom they had received the blessing. Only one of them recognized his obli-gation to be grateful for the gift which he had received. And before going further he parted company with the nine, turned back, and when he had found Jesus, fell at his feet and poured out the gratitude of his heart for the blessing bestowed. The nine pass into obscurity; the one enters into immortality. We do not know his name,—we hear only of his fame. "And he was a Samaritan." Let us call him the better Samaritan.

II

The better Samaritan would teach us that gratitude does not depend upon the state of one's health, but upon the condition of one's heart. The case of the nine demonstrates the fact that it does not follow that a miracle of healing will cause the recipient to become "lost in wonder, love, and praise." Apparently they were entirely forgetful of gratitude, or totally lacking in that quality of life. With words that stab and sting,

Paul characterizes the ungrateful: "Neither were [they] thankful; but became vain in their imaginations, and their foolish heart was darkened." Just so! no novelist or dramatist could have characterized more accurately the blighting effect of ingratitude.

No, gratitude does not depend upon the condition of one's health. Neither sickness nor suffering, adversity nor misfortune can put to silence a song of gratitude if the "heart keeps right."

It often happens that what appears to be a misfortune is simply one of God's blessings in disguise. Said the psalmist, "Before I was afflicted I went astray: but now have I kept thy word. . . . It is good for me that I have been afflicted."

No one has provided better proof of this truth than the Apostle Paul, who bore in his body the marks of the Lord Jesus. His body was welted with cruel whippings and scarred with severe persecutions. Besides, he had a thorn in the flesh. "For this thing," says he, "I besought the Lord thrice, that it might depart from me." But it remained. The only answer God gave to his thrice-repeated prayer was, "My grace is sufficient for thee: for my strength is made perfect in weakness." God did not remove the thorn in the flesh, but he did give him strength with which to "bear the strain of toil, the fret of care." Therefore, with a shout of joy in his heart and a paean of praise on his tongue, we hear him declare, "Most gladly therefore will I rather glory in my infirmities, that the power of Christ may rest upon me."

Moreover, this spirit is strikingly illustrated by Reverend Martin Rinkert, who lived in a day of extreme

privation and hardship. The Thirty Years' War in
his native land had impoverished and inflicted extreme
hardships on the people. "So great were Rinkert's own
losses and charities that he had utmost difficulty in
finding bread and clothes for his children." To add
to the woes brought on by the war, a terrible epidemic
stalked through the land, and Rinkert buried so many
people that a man of less faith would have been filled
with fear and futility. Certainly by all outward tokens
he should have been singing a dirge or a lamentation
instead of a hymn of thanksgiving. But he illustrates
the undeniable fact that it is out of the abundance
of the heart and not because of the robustness of the
health that man sings his songs of praise. For, amidst
want and woe, sickness and death, sorrow and suffering, he wrote,

> Now thank we all our God
>   With hearts and hands and voices,
> Who wondrous things hath done,
>   In whom his world rejoices;
> Who, from our mothers' arms
>   Hath blessed us on our way
> With countless gifts of love,
>   And still is ours today.[1]

III

Again, the better Samaritan would teach us that
gratitude does not depend upon what one has in the
hand, but upon what one has in the heart. It is out
of the abundance of the heart, and not because of the
opulence of the harvest, that man sings a song of
thanksgiving to God. History and experience offer

---

[1] By permission of Willett, Clark & Co., Chicago.

ample proof of the contention that gratitude does not depend upon prosperity or poverty, but upon the inner springs of life.

Our first national Thanksgiving was an acknowledgment of a very frugal harvest amid manifold dangers and multiplied privations. It was a day of "big thanks" for "little favors." Today, it is just the opposite: "little thanks" for "big favors." Never was our country more bountifully blessed; and never were we less truly thankful. We grow more greedy and grasping instead of more grateful and God-fearing.

Gratitude does not depend upon things. One cannot satisfy the soul with stocks and securities. The more a man gets, the more he wants. However, a man's life does not consist in the abundance of things which he possesses, but in his attitude and relationship to God from whom all blessings flow. In recent years there are some who have become sullen and sour in spirit because they have been taught to cast covetous eyes upon the things which others have. As a result they have become envious. They are a great deal like the psalmist who confesses, "My feet were almost gone; my steps had well nigh slipped. For I was envious at the foolish, when I saw the prosperity of the wicked." That is the danger when one covets the possessions of others. Somewhere I read the story of a saintly man who went window shopping through the business section of New York City. Late in the evening, worn and weary, he returned to his room. Before retiring, he kneeled to pray, saying, "Lord, I thank thee that there are so many things I do not want."

The truly grateful are those who look not at what they lack, but at what they have; therefore, they can sing,

> Count your many blessings,
> Name them one by one,
> And it will surprise you
> What the Lord hath done.

Try turning your thoughts from what you lack to what you have. After hearing a Thanksgiving sermon, a good deacon said to me, "I am thankful for the things I do not have: for the things that did not happen to me." In a day when the most destructive and devastating war in human history stalks through the world like a deadly plague, when human liberty and religious freedom have been lost to merciless dictators who keep their neighbors in perpetual fear of what may happen next, we can be truly "thankful for what did not happen" to us; thankful that we live in a land where liberty and human are still cherished and honored. But let us not forget that we have political freedom and religious liberty because of the sacrificial price paid by our forefathers, and that there rests upon us the sacred responsibility of preserving for posterity the precious heritage bequeathed to us.

IV

Yet again, the better Samaritan would teach us that gratitude depends upon humility of heart and not upon the abundance of the harvest. The humble are thankful; the haughty are thankless. There is no denying the fact that there is a haughty spirit abroad in the land today. Many have a quarrel with life because they secretly cherish the feeling that they have been cheated and deprived of all that should have come to them. If you feel that you deserve a better world in which to live, then help to make it so. Selfish greed and a haughty spirit have made the world what it is today. Answer aright the question, How much of the bounty which God has bestowed have I actually earned or rightly deserved? and you will feel very humble and grateful.

The humble hearted Samaritan returned to offer gratitude to God for what Christ had done for him because he had a feeling that he had neither earned nor merited the blessing which he had received. The nine ungrateful Jews, with their racial pride and prejudice, parted company with the despised Samaritan once they were cured of the disease which had made them his companions. The nine were healed in body, but were still indifferent and lacking in gratitude. The one was healed in body, spirit, and soul. Therefore, with gratitude in his heart he sang,

> He cleansed, and thus made me whole
>   In body, mind, spirit, and soul.
> All praise to His name!
>   I'll sing of His fame,
> While the ages of eternity roll.

We are all beneficiaries of God. He sent his Son to rescue us from the stronghold of Satan. "God so loved the world, that he gave his only begotten Son, that whosoever believeth in him should not perish, but have everlasting life." We have greater reason to be grateful to God than the Samaritan had, but we do little or nothing about it.

The psalmist, after enumerating the many blessings which he had received as a beneficiary of God, asked himself the question, "What shall I render unto the Lord for all his benefits toward me?" And then to his question he replies, "I will take the cup of salvation, and call upon the name of the Lord. I will pay my vows unto the Lord now in the presence of all his people." That is, I will make public acknowledgment of my gratitude to God by taking the cup of salvation which he has proffered.

That is the sort of gratitude and thanksgiving which every soul should express to God for the gift of his Son. If you have not already taken the cup of salvation which God has provided in his Son, I invite and urge you to take it now "in the presence of all his people . . . in the courts of the Lord's house." I bid you

> Come to Christ, confession make;
> Come to Christ and pardon take.

IX

BORDERLAND BAPTISTS

Wherefore, said they, if we have found grace in thy sight, let this land be given unto thy servants for a possession, and bring us not over Jordan.—NUMBERS 32: 5.

I

In their journey from the land of bondage, the Israelites, "with painful steps and slow," came, at last, to the border of the land of promise. Very shortly they would cross over and begin the conquest of Canaan. However, at this juncture the children of Reuben and the children of Gad came forward with a disturbing and a disquieting request: "Let this land be given us for a possession, and bring us not over Jordan."

To their petition Moses replied, "Shall your brethren go to war, and shall ye sit here?" This question was not propounded to Reuben and Gad for purposes of debate; neither did Moses expect nor even wait for a reply. From the tone of his voice and the accent of his words there was no mistaking his meaning. He had a hero's contempt for the craven cowardice and the sordid selfishness inherent in the request which they had made. If Moses had put into speech what he felt in his spirit, doubtless he would have said: "You contemptible cowards! Shall you sit here sheltered from hardships while your brethren go to war? No! you will do nothing of the kind. You will accompany them or be court-martialed and stoned to death for treason!"

The sin of which Reuben and Gad were guilty was the sin of disloyalty to comrades in conquest and indifference to pledged duty. They were under solemn covenant to accompany their brethren in battle; but instead, they begged, "Bring us not over Jordan." Let us remain in the land of Gilead and Jazer, sheltered from the privations and sacrifices consequent to the conquest of Canaan. Moses knew that if such a selfishness were tolerated it would have a blighting effect upon the spirit of the people: "Wherefore," said he, "discourage ye the heart of the children of Israel from going over into the land which the Lord hath given them?"

As is so often true, Moses knew that it was a case of "hanging together or hanging separately." Therefore he made it clear that responsibility in life goes far beyond the range of personal preference. Reuben and Gad might sit still while their brethren went to war and not experience any very great harm to themselves; but their example would have a very detrimental effect upon the morale of their brethren. To make this truth sink into their forgetful minds and selfish hearts, Moses rehearsed in their ears a bit of history. Said he in effect: "Thus did your fathers, when I sent them from Kadesh-barnea to see the land. They came back saying that it couldn't be done; that they were not able to go up and possess the land; that it was inhabited by giants, the sons of Anak; that we were in our own sight as grasshoppers, and so we were in their sight. Thus they discouraged the hearts of the children of Israel with the result that they wandered in the wilderness for forty years. Your attitude proves that you are the direct descendants of the ten whose report brought disaster upon the children of Israel. You should remember that we are all bound up in the bundle of life together. The calamity you bring upon your brethren by your sin of disloyalty and indifference, you will surely bring upon yourselves."

Thus Moses persuaded the past to speak to the present. He called forth fathers long since dead and bade them rise up and speak to living sons, warning them against repeating the sin which they themselves had committed. "If you will not go to war with your brethren," said Moses, "behold, you have sinned against the Lord: and be sure your sins will find you out. . . . For if you turn away from God, he will yet again leave us in the wilderness, and you shall destroy all this people." In this graphic manner he pointed out to Reuben and Gad the ponderable fact that their sin was not only a sin against their kindred, but a sin against God as well.

There is no denying the fact that attitudes and actions of men have far-reaching social consequences. It is not possible for a professing Christian to say, "I will not join my brethren in public worship on the Lord's day; instead, I will go out into the wide open spaces and worship God under the blue sky," without his example having a harmful effect on others. In the Old Testament there is a story of a king, Jotham by name, of whom it is said, "And he did that which was right in the eyes of Jehovah, according to all that his father Uzziah had done: howbeit he entered not into the temple of Jehovah" (ASV). Then in one brief sentence the writer sums up the far-reaching social consequences of Jotham's bad example: "And the people did yet corruptly." He might stay away from the sanctuary on the sabbath day without any very great harm to himself; but not so with those who followed his example. They lacked the moral stamina which he possessed. The full tragedy of Jotham's example came to fruition in his son Ahaz, who succeeded him as king and followed his example of not entering into the sanctuary on the sabbath. He became so vile in his private and public life that he was not permitted burial in the sepulcher of the kings.

II

Always in any moral or spiritual conquest there are some who will be loyal within certain limits, who will do their duty to a degree; but beyond that they are not to be relied upon. It is even so with many who join the crusade for Christ. They will go so far and then, either by word or deed, beg to be allowed to dwell on the borderland of sacrificial service and self-denial. It was so in Paul's day. Like Moses, he, too, had to deal with those who were disloyal to their brethren and indifferent to their duty. To all such lovers of ease and dodgers of duty he said, "Take your share of hardships as good soldiers of Jesus Christ."

The Reubenites and the Gadites with whom Moses and Paul had to deal are still with us. The spirit of these ancient citizens has found its way into our churches today. As a result we have a host of borderland Baptists—church members who live on the fringe of religious reality, shirking every duty and shunning all responsibility. A recent survey of the churches of our denomination brought forth the distressing facts that 47 per cent of the membership of our churches are names only; 54 per cent give nothing; and another sizeable number, 25 per cent, are non-resident. These are our borderland Baptists, followers of Reuben and Gad. In a former pastorate I found a typical example of these tribes. He claimed to be a Christian, and a Baptist by choice; but he steadfastly refused to unite with the church. In the hope of winning him to active membership, he was elected superintendent of our Bible school. In due time I approached him and asked for a definite committal of his allegiance to the church, and received the reply, "I am a public servant, and feel that I should not show partiality in matters of religion by joining any particular church." Some weeks after that a former pastor came to town. Because he was a man of experience, I told him my story and asked his advice. "Well," said he, "if I were pastor here, I would prefer that he live on the other side of the hill. When I was pastor here he was in turn superintendent of public schools and postmaster, and his excuse for not joining the church then was the same as that given you." At the time I was trying to win him for the church, he was editor of a paper with a particular political slant. But he failed to see that there was any inconsistency in his reason for not joining the church and his being an avowed partisan in politics, holding office at the hands of his party, and editing a paper in its behalf. I finally came to the conclusion that he was just another borderland Baptist, one who shared the blessings and benefits of religion and the church, but unwilling to assume any responsibility for the privileges he enjoyed. Very soon my feeling toward him was similar to that expressed by the former pastor. Certainly we lose our respect for the man who tries to play fast and loose, who does not have the courage to stand up for what he professes to believe.

In a day when so many professed followers of Christ are shirking their share of the hardships common to the Christian conquest, we need to hear again the admonition of Paul, "Take your share of hardships as good soldiers of Christ." We who have joined that particular company of believers called Baptists should remember that our covenant is not with our brethren alone; we have entered into a solemn and sacred covenant with God the Father and Jesus Christ, his Son. Failure to be loyal soldiers in the worldwide conquest for the enthronement of our Lord and King, is not only a sin against fellow believers, it is treason against our Lord and King.

We need to be reminded that Christianity proclaims the doctrine of the democracy of responsibility as well as the doctrine of the democracy of privilege. As Baptists, we are accustomed to hear a great deal about the democracy of privilege, the rights, worth, and value of the individual. We declare that a Baptist church is composed of "baptized believers, equal in rank and privilege." But we seem to have forgotten the biblical doctrine of the democracy of responsibility. Time and again the summons has gone forth, calling the followers of Christ to "Come up to the help of the Lord, to the help of the Lord against the mighty." But alas! many never heed the call. They prefer to remain at ease in the land adjacent to the territory where the real conquest for Christ is being waged.

However, none of us can boast of doing his full duty and living up to the maximum requirements of the faith we profess. Frequently I find myself praying,

> In that I have so greatly failed Thee, Lord,
>   Have grace!
>
> . . . .
>
> So much of what I might have done, I did not do.

In much this way the Apostle Paul felt as he compared his accomplishments with what he hoped to do, or might have done. If ever there was a man who might have been content with his accomplishments, it was Paul. But instead, we hear him declare, "Not as though I had already attained, either were already perfect: . . . but this one thing I do, forgetting those things which are behind, and reaching forth unto those things which are before, I press toward the mark for the prize of the high calling of God in Christ Jesus."

Nevertheless, there is a vast difference between failing because of indifference to duty, and falling short of full performance because of lack of time or opportunity. The one is failure for lack of effort; the other is failure in spite of honest endeavor. And we have the assurance that God credits us with the will to do, and the effort to achieve, though we may fall short of success; for to one who failed to bring to consummation a life-long dream, we hear him say, "Thou didst well in that it was in thine heart." It was wanton failure, failure for lack of effort, as in the case of the one-talent man, that Christ condemned: "Thou wicked and slothful servant, . . . Take therefore the talent from him, . . .

And cast ye the unprofitable servant into outer darkness: there shall be weeping and gnashing of teeth."

> Must I go, and empty-handed,
>   Thus my dear Redeemer meet?
> Not one day of service give Him
>   Lay no trophy at His feet?

III

We need not overlook the fact that the Reubenites and the Gadites were respectable folk, the blood kinsmen of that loyal company who stood ready to cross over Jordan and begin the conquest of Canaan. And the multitude of borderland Baptists about whom we have been speaking are, for the most part, respectable —our relatives, friends, and neighbors. Their chief sin is that they have settled down in ease just outside the territory where the conquest for Christ is being waged. Most of them refrain from overt acts of sensual sin; but they cannot summon sufficient courage to take an uncompromising stand

> In the strife of truth with falsehood,
> For the good or evil side.

There are those who are loud in the affirmation that they are Baptists. They will tell you so with a certain degree of pride. But once you undertake to persuade them to perform the part of loyal Baptists, to co-operate with their brethren in carrying the Christian conquest into the territory of the enemy, you find that they are mere borderland Baptists. They dwell close enough to the realities of religion to share the blessings and benefits which accrue from the activities of the faithful few; but they are unwilling to assume any of the responsibilities which such blessings and privileges entail. They are content to live in the land adjacent to the territory in which a battle royal is being waged for the Redeemer of men.

A mother, a member of my church, betrayed the fact that she was one of this considerable number when in protest against some religious requirements for her children she said, "I do not want my children to become too religious." All she required for herself and her children was that they be permitted to dwell near enough to the realities of religion to share the blessings and benefits without assuming any of the responsibilities which such privileges require. But the tragedy of such an attitude is that it denies one the discipline necessary for the development of his character and spiritual life. And any mother who takes such an attitude will soon find her children deserting the church, religion, and God. For he who tries to be a half Christian soon becomes a confirmed pagan.

And yet, what one of these "marginal members," borderland Baptists, would not storm the heights if the church should depart from her historic stand on immersion as the true New Testament form of baptism? They seem to forget, if indeed they ever knew, that Christ had immensely more to say about stewardship than he did about baptism. But undertake to persuade them to practice Christ's teachings on stewardship and you find them as cold and callous as an Egyptian mummy. In the absence of the pastor, Dr. Austin Crouch was asked to supply the pulpit of one of the greatest churches in the Southern Baptist Convention. He began his sermon thus, "How many of you will promise to find out all Christ had to say about baptism, and will do exactly what he said?" In response, every hand went up. Then Dr. Crouch countered, "How many of you will promise to find out all Christ said about stewardship, and will do exactly what he said?" Only a few hands went up.

Just so! The cause of Christ is not suffering for want of recruits, but for lack of consecration on the part of those who profess to believe in his name. If his cause ever suffers defeat, it will be at the instigation of that large number of professed followers who, like the Reubenites and the Gadites, are disloyal to their brethren, indifferent to their duty, and unfaithful to their Lord. We hear a great deal today about the sin of wrongdoing; but a more deadly sin besets the followers of Christ: the sin of doing very little or nothing.

To many professed followers of Christ there are no sharply drawn issues between right and wrong. As for them, a truce has been declared, an armistice has been signed, and the forces which should be hostile to each other are mingling peaceably, with the result that the one cannot be distinguished from the other. If evil were an honorable thing, such an attitude might be tolerable. But evil is an enemy, an intruder. Its purpose is to rob, to steal, to pillage, and to destroy. To be indifferent in the strife of truth with falsehood is to play the part of a traitor to the cause, and leave it to others to fight our battle for us. What would you think of a citizen who was utterly indifferent toward an enemy who was invading his country, destroying property, and murdering women and little children? There is no word, or combination of words, in the English language that would adequately express your feeling of contempt. Yet, how much better is he who professes to be a follower of Christ and is utterly indifferent toward the evil that stalks about the country of his King, destroying Christian ideals and institutions, and blighting the lives and damning the souls of men? There is no neutral ground for a Christian. There is but one side on which he should take his stand, and that is the side of right. When a Christian beholds the havoc that evil has wrought, the hearts it has broken, the homes it has destroyed, the hopes it has blighted, the virtue it has blasted, the suffering it has caused, he should

> Loathe it in his bosom,
> Scorn it with his eyes,
> Hate it with his latest breath
> And fight it till he dies.

One of the chief weaknesses of our denomination—all denominations for that matter—is that the spirit of Reuben and Gad pervades our ranks. The next great revival must be the evangelization of that great host of marginal members and borderland Christians. If you are a borderland Baptist, a marginal Methodist, a lukewarm Lutheran, a pharisaical Presbyterian, an ephemeral Episcopalian, let this old story stir you out of your complacent indifference and send you forth into the conflict for Christ. Then shall we be able to sing,

Like a mighty army
  Moves the Church of God;
Brothers, we are treading
  Where the saints have trod;
We are not divided,
  All one body we,
One in hope and doctrine,
  One in charity.

Crowns and thrones may perish,
  Kingdoms rise and wane;
But the Church of Jesus
  Constant will remain;
Gates of hell can never
  'Gainst that Church prevail;
We have Christ's own promise—
  And that cannot fail.

X

THE NEW FISHING FIRM

And Jesus said unto Simon, Fear not; from henceforth thou shalt catch men.—LUKE 5:10.

I

Long ago, over one of the stalls in the market place in Capernaum, there may have been seen the inscription,

PETER, ZEBEDEE, AND SONS

For these men were partner fishermen. However, the day came when there were no fish on sale at the market of this particular firm. They had toiled all night and had taken nothing. A few more nights of failure and across their place of business, in large bold letters, would be written,

FAILED! GONE OUT OF BUSINESS

But sunup found the undefeated fishermen making ready for another effort. At an early hour they were bending their backs to the task of washing and mending their nets. Maybe the filthy condition of the nets had caused the fish to evade them, or the broken strands of the nets had allowed the fish to escape them. While thus engaged, Jesus came along followed by a multitude hungry for the gracious words that fell from his lips. Thereupon, he approached Peter and asked for the privilege of using his boat for a pulpit from which to preach to the people. The request being granted, "He entered into one of the ships, which was Simon's, and prayed him that he would thrust out a little from the land. And he sat down, and taught the people out of the ship." When Peter loaned his boat for a pulpit and began to co-operate with Jesus in securing for him a more advantageous position from which to preach the Word to the waiting throng, the old partnership of Peter, Zebedee, and Sons became the New Fishing Firm,

JESUS,
PETER, AND ZEBEDEE'S SONS

Now that Jesus was head of the firm, it was evident that some radical changes would have to be made. To begin with, the boat with which Peter and his partners had failed in their all night quest for daily food was being used to dispense Bread that would satisfy the hungry souls of men and win them for the kingdom of God. The fish the old partnership had been catching had been the daily diet of the people, and a daily recurring necessity. Henceforth the fishermen were to be partners with one who was a dispenser of the Bread of Life.

> Break Thou the bread of life,
>   Dear Lord, to me,
> As Thou didst break the loaves
>   Beside the sea;
> Beyond the sacred page
>   I seek Thee, Lord;
> My spirit pants for Thee,
>   O living Word.
>
> Thou art the bread of life,
>   O Lord, to me,
> Thy holy Word the truth
>   That saveth me;
> Give me to eat and live
>   With Thee above;
> Teach me to love Thy truth,
>   For Thou art love.

The next change made by the head of the new fishing firm is comprehended in the command, "Launch out into the deep, and let down your nets for a draught." Compliance with this command called for a radical departure from the methods employed by the old firm of Peter, Zebedee, and Sons. It required a change contrary to tradition, and to the experience of skilled fishermen. But it was nothing unusual for Jesus to break with old customs and traditions and launch out upon an entirely new course of conduct. Repeatedly he declared, "Ye have heard that it was said by them of old time. . . . But I say unto you. . . ." Not infrequently he makes requests and exacts requirements that seem radical and unreasonable to business executives and industrialists today. Many have not found the faith, the vision, and the courage to adopt his way in business and industry. The few who have, have found in him their greatest boon and benefit. The firm that has the faith, the vision, and the courage to give the people something more than can be wrapped up in paper, that can deliver its product with the stamp of the Golden Rule upon it, will have its place of operation thronged with customers eager to receive the valuable merchandise it has to offer.

II

When Jesus called upon Peter to launch out into the deep and let down his net for a draught, he was asking for more than the use of his boat: he was exacting full co-operation and implicit obedience. Without hesitation or protest, Peter was ready to lend his boat for a pulpit. By thrusting out a little from the land, he manifested his willingness to assist the Master in securing a more advantageous position from which to preach to "the people pressed upon him to hear the word of God." But when called upon to co-operate and to give full obedience to the unreasonable command to launch out into the deep in broad daylight, contrary to experience and seasoned judgment of skilled fishermen, he registered his protest and showed his lack of faith in the wisdom of the new management. To lend his boat for a pulpit from which the Word of God might be proclaimed was one thing; but to lend himself to such a new and novel method was quite another. Jesus of Nazareth might know the art of preaching, but, in the opinion of Peter, it did not follow that he knew equally well the art of fishing.

The spirit of Peter is still with us. There are not a few who count Jesus supreme as a religious teacher; but in matters of business he is impracticable. There are those who can sit in the pew and listen with rapture to his teachings so long as the application is kept impersonal. But when a preacher makes it clear that Christ requires that his principles be practiced in social, domestic, economic, and public life as well as in private, he is likely to get himself labeled as a communist and be asked to resign. There are those who are willing to give him some of their ill-gotten gold, willing to launch out a bit if by doing so they may assist him in securing a more advantageous position from which he may preach to the people. The people need religion to keep them patient and docile in spite of maladjusted social and economic conditions. But when a pastor asks these men of privilege to assume full responsibility of their stewardship, make an unconditional surrender to Christ,

and give full obedience to his Word, not a few, like the
rich young ruler, go away sorrowfully, if not angrily.

Besides the fact that the command of Christ was
contrary to well-established methods, experienced fishermen had failed in the waters to which he was ordering
a return. With a wave of the hand Peter said, "Master,
we have toiled all the night [out there], and have taken
nothing." Perhaps, Peter thought that his protest
would produce a change of mind on the part of the
manager of the new firm. But instead, Christ was
more persistent: "Launch out into the deep, and let
down your nets for a draught." Thereupon Peter re-
luctantly yielded saying, "Nevertheless at thy word
I will let down the net." It was as if Peter had said:
"Master, if against all odds you insist, very well, I
will obey; but only at thy word. You shall be responsible for the outcome of the venture." And well
he might! as the results clearly show; for "they in-
closed a great multitude of fishes: and their net brake.
And they beckoned unto their partners, which were in
the other ship, that they should come and help them."

Moreover, when Jesus called upon Peter and his partners to "Launch out into the deep, and let down your
nets for a draught," he was calling for a venture of
faith, for operation in deeper waters, and for wider
circles of usefulness. But to begin to enlarge and expand right in the face of failure was a tremendous
venture for men of little faith. They were not yet
aware of the deep waters into which they had been led
by complying with the request that they lend their boat
for a pulpit. But having gone thus far, Jesus seemed
to be saying to them: "Get ye out into deeper waters

where demands will be made upon your faith, where all your resources will be utilized, and where every member of the partnership will be called upon to cooperate to the full extent of his ability." And it was so. For "when they had this done," the results were so astounding that "they beckoned unto their partners, which were in the other ship, that they should come and help them. And they came, and filled both the ships, so that they began to sink."

The reply of Peter, "Nevertheless at thy word I will let down the net," has been interpreted by some as an expression of faith and obedience. Evidently this interpretation is made in the light of subsequent events rather than in the full light of the immediate circumstance. We should remember that Peter was the hardheaded, self-willed, impulsive and cursing type of fisherman. He was a man who would not readily take to new and novel methods in his lifelong business. He had an air about him which seemed to say, "When I have failed, there is no use in anyone else trying." It was as if he had said, "I will show you that you do not know what you are talking about." It was in that sort of mood that Peter put out into the deep. He had the sort of contempt for the orders of the Teacher that some laymen have for the business judgment of the preacher. Peter scarcely knew Jesus at the time. How could he be expected to adopt such untried methods solely on faith?

Besides, the argument that it was in an attitude of faith and obedience that Peter put out into the deep is all out of harmony with the complete astonishment manifested on the part of Peter and his partners. "For

he was astonished, and all that were with him, at the
draught of fishes which they had taken: and so also
were James, and John, the sons of Zebedee, which were
partners with Simon." Faith never reacts like that.
Faith is always expectant and never amazed at results.
It goes to work believing that it is going to succeed
and realize its full expectations. But here was a man
who was astonished and amazed at the results. At the
sight of the draught of fishes Peter made an open
confession and offered an apology for the lack of faith
he had shown, for the tone of voice he had used when
he replied to Jesus' command to launch out into the
deep. "When Simon Peter saw it, he fell down at
Jesus' knees, saying, Depart from me; for I am a sinful man, O Lord." In his poem, "The Master of My
Boat," Joseph Addison Richards has expressed the
change that took place in the attitude of Peter:

> I owned a little boat awhile ago
>   And sailed a Morning Sea without a fear,
> And whither any breeze might fairly blow
>   I'd steer the little craft afar or near.
>   Mine was the boat,
>   And mine the air,
>   And mine the sea,
>   Not mine a care.
>
> My boat became my place of nightly toil,
>   I sailed at sunset to the fishing ground;
> At morn my boat was freighted with the spoil
>   That my all-conquering work and skill had found.
>   Mine was the boat,
>   And mine the net,
>   And mine the skill
>   And power to get.

One day there passed along the silent shore,
  While I my net was casting in the sea,
A Man, who spoke as never man before;
  I followed Him—new life began in me.
    Mine was the boat,
      But His the voice,
    And His the call,
      Yet mine the choice.

Ah, 'twas a fearful night out on the lake,
  And all my skill availed not at the helm,
Till Him asleep I waken, crying, "Take,
  Take Thou command, lest waters overwhelm!"
    His was the boat,
      And His the sea,
    And His the peace
      O'er all and me.

Once from His boat He taught the curious throng,
  Then bade me let down nets out in the sea;
I murmured, but obeyed, nor was it long
  Before the catch amazed and humbled me.
    His was the boat,
      And His the skill,
    And His the catch,
      And His my will.[1]

                              —JOSEPH ADDISON RICHARDS

Therefore, we conclude that it was not so much a matter of faith as it was the fact of failure that caused Peter to obey the Master's orders. Failure, if complete enough, puts a man in an attitude of being willing to receive and act upon suggestions, though he may doubt the wisdom of the same. Peter and his partners had failed, exhausted their resources in an all night fruitless effort. Jesus came along in the early hour of failure

[1]By permission of Willett, Clark & Co., Chicago.

with a suggestion that was contrary to the tradition of their trade. I dare say that not a single member of the firm was favorably impressed. But failure, and the authoritative tone of the Master's voice, seemed to impel them to obey. They did, and the results justified the Master's method, though different from that hitherto employed by Peter, Zebedee, and Sons.

III

Given a partnership with the faith, the vision, and the courage to make Jesus head of the firm, and success is inevitable. One of the best modern examples of this truth is the story of the A. Nash Company, of Cincinnati. The partnership had been toiling for months and taking nothing. The head of the firm had made up his mind to close out his business, and was working toward that end. While thus engaged something unusual happened. One of the pastors of the city asked Mr. Nash to occupy his pulpit. Mr. Nash warned him that, though he at one time had been a minister, he had lost his faith and was an agnostic and a confirmed skeptic. But the pastor insisted, and Mr. Nash accepted. He said that he made up his mind to prepare and preach a sermon that would disprove the teachings of the Sermon on the Mount. But in making a thorough study of the Sermon on the Mount, he came to the conclusion that it had never been tried. The result was that he went into the pulpit as a defender of the teachings of Jesus. Moreover, he determined that he would undertake to operate his business according to the principle set forth in the Golden Rule. He went before his employees and announced to them his plan, and asked for their co-operation. He got it with enthusiasm; and instead of closing out it soon became necessary for him to expand.

In an hour of near failure, Jesus came along and asked for the opportunity and privilege of using the A. Nash Clothing Company as a pulpit from which to proclaim the teachings of Jesus. The head of the firm gave his consent. Then and there new life entered the industry. All plans for closing were abandoned. Very soon the volume of business increased to the extent that larger quarters had to be secured, and a call had to be sent out for more help. It was as if the failing firm had heard Jesus say, "Launch out into the deep, and let down your nets for a draught." The results were that thousands of dollars were shared with the employees. All of which should teach us that Jesus knows how to manage a fishing firm, a clothing industry, a steel mill, or a machine shop. If capital would make Jesus its controlling partner, and labor would elect him as its leader, crippled industry would get on its feet, strikes and strife would cease, and business would flourish.

The success which crowned that day's work out there on the lake was neither the end nor the chief business of the new fishing firm. That day the new manager declared, "Fear not; from henceforth thou shalt catch men. And when they had brought their ships to land, they forsook all, and followed him." No longer would the fishing grounds be limited by the narrow confines of the Sea of Galilee. Henceforth the world would be the field of endeavor: "Go ye into all the world," said the head of the firm, "and preach the gospel to every creature." "Launch out into the deep, and let down your nets for a draught." One of the men who heard and heeded the command, made a catch of three thousand in one day: "And the same day there were added to the church about three thousand souls."

Since that day the new fishing firm has grown into a partnership of millions. And to every partner of the firm there comes the command, "Fear not; from henceforth thou shalt catch men." Launch out into the deep waters of Christian experience where demands will be made on faith, where the results will strain to the breaking point all resources, and where every member of the partnership will be called upon to co-operate to the full extent of his ability. Go ye into all the world, and preach the gospel to every creature.

> The livelong night we've toiled in vain,
> But at Thy gracious word,
> We will let down the net again,—
> Do Thou Thy will, O Lord.

XI

"YOUNG MAN, . . . ARISE"

Young man, I say unto thee, Arise. And he that was dead sat up, and began to speak. And he delivered him to his mother.— Luke 7 : 14-15.

I

Long ago, in the ancient city of Nain, there lived a little family of three: father, mother, and son. But before the sacred scribe started to write their story the grim reaper of death had already garnered the head of the house. And now the son had been summoned "to join the innumerable caravan, which moves to that mysterious realm, where each shall take his chamber in the silent halls of death." Therefore, the sad scene which greets our eyes is a funeral procession. A widowed mother is following the bier of her boy.

But the unusual and the unexpected happened! The procession was met in the way by Jesus who "touched the bier: and they that bare him stood still. And he said, Young man, I say unto thee, Arise. And he that was dead sat up, and began to speak. And he delivered him to his mother."

HOW IS A MOTHER BEREAVED OF HER BOY?

Many a mother is bereaved of her boy, not because he has departed this life physically, but because he has wilfully gone out of her life to go the way of the world. Jesus makes this truth stand out distinctly in his parable of the prodigal son. In this case, to be sure, it was a father instead of a mother who was bereaved of his boy. But that does not alter the fundamental truth. The son had wilfully gone out of his father's life to walk in the counsel of the ungodly, to stand in the way with sinners, and to sit in the seat of the scornful. And as a result the father said, "This my son was dead." Even so a mother is bereaved of her boy when he wilfully goes out of her life and becomes insensible to her hopes, indifferent to her prayers, and careless of her love and tears.

But what is it more than all else besides that bereaves a mother of her boy, that takes him out of her life to go the way of worldlings? It is the company he keeps. Here was a young man who was being carried away from his mother by his companions. But you will say: "Oh, that is different! This young man was unaware of what his friends were doing. He was dead. His friends were performing the part of pallbearers." That is just the point! It is always true of him who is being carried away by evil companions! He is insensible to what is really happening and unaware of the end to which he is being carried. Indeed the most common cause of a young man's moral decease is the company he keeps. In the end, evil companions always prove to be his pallbearers.

To be sure a young man never intends that his friends shall become the pallbearers of his moral decease. But they are the very folk who most frequently serve in that capacity. Here, for example, is the story of a young man of my acquaintance. For a time he was a comfort and the only support of his widowed mother. He was a son of promise and the pride of a fond mother. Then a subtle change came over him. At first his mother was unable to fathom the cause. But ere long she learned that evil companions had cast a spell over him and were carrying him off to his moral ruin. He took to drinking and joy-riding. One night while out on a wild ride with his companions their car was wrecked and he was killed. When a young man's companions have brought about his moral decease, they have also begun to dig a pit into which to cast his dissipated body. If only a young man could look down the road upon which he has entered with evil companions and see at the end of the way the woe that awaits him, surely he would not continue to follow in their train or to keep company with them. "My son, if sinners entice thee, consent thou not. . . . Walk thou not in the way with them; refrain thy foot from their path: for their feet run to evil, and make haste to shed blood."

If only a son could realize, before it is eternally too late, that Mother is his best friend, certainly he would not allow evil companions to tear him from her bosom and carry him off to his moral ruin. Remember, son, Mother is mainly interested in what she can put into you and make out of you; others are primarily interested in what they can get out of you. Witness how the prodigal's friends pillaged him and then discarded him when he had spent all his living. But alas! how many sons there are who go out of Mother's life and join themselves to companions whose chief interest is to exploit and rob them of life's richest treasure—character! And the tragedy of it is that so often mothers are not able to prevent it. For sons of the best of mothers go astray. But, sad to relate, the fact is that not every mother's influence is what it should be.

WHAT MAY A MOTHER DO?

In the second place, what is there that a mother may do to prevent the loss of her son to the influence of evil companions? The only real preventive at her disposal is to have Jesus present in her heart and home. How did it happen that friends of this widow's son got started on their way with him to an open grave? Jesus was not present to prevent it. Like Martha and Mary, this mother might well have said, "Lord, if thou hadst been here, my son had not died." He was in the vicinity, but that did not suffice. Nor will it today. And yet, how many there are who seem to think that all that is necessary is to live within calling distance of the Lord. They have no need of him except in cases of emergency. There are those who treat Christ as they do their family physician: they call on him in cases of extreme need, and then dismiss him without pay, praise, or gratitude. The psalmist expressed the attitude of all too many folk when he said: "The sorrows of death compassed me, and the pains of hell gat hold upon me: I found trouble and sorrow. Then called I upon the name of the Lord; O Lord, I beseech thee, deliver my soul." All too many of us wait until "the sorrows of death" compass us. God is no mere emergency God. He must be our refuge in time of peace if we expect to find in him our strength and help in time of trouble.

But what is a mother to do once evil companions are on their way with her boy? How shall she stop the procession once it has started? How shall a mother save her son and reclaim him for her own heart and hopes? There is but one way: the procession must be met in the way by Jesus. He alone is able to stop a son who is on the downward road to ruin. He is always traveling in the opposite direction. Ever since the resurrection morning Christ has been traveling the triumphant road. When he meets a young man on his way to his moral grave, he says, "Young man, I say unto thee, Arise."

Let us not forget that one of the principal factors in bringing about the timely meeting of a son with the Saviour is a mother's prayers. In this sad story of a mother following the bier of her boy, the first thing that arrested the attention of the Master and caused him to call a halt was the sight of the heartbroken mother. "And when the Lord saw her, he had compassion on her, and said unto her, Weep not. And he came and touched the bier: and they that bare him stood still. And he said, Young man, I say unto thee, Arise. And he that was dead sat up, and began to speak. And he delivered him to his mother."

Mother, here is hope and a promise for you! It may be that in response to your prayers the Master will meet your wayward son on his downward way and give him back to you, a new creature in Christ. Therefore, pursue him with your prayers! He may be on the last lap of the way to the open grave where your one remaining ray of hope will be interred. Follow him with your prayers! It may be that Jesus will meet him, stay and restore him to you, "clothed and in his right mind." The key to your son's salvation may be prayer. Use it! There is not in all literature a more beautiful story of the redeeming power of a mother's prayers than that of Monica praying for her prodigal son, Augustine. With-

out stint or restraint he was giving himself to every
pleasure and vice under the sun, while his mother
pleaded with him to mend his ways. At last he decided
to go to Rome that, far beyond the prayers and admoni-
tions of his mother, he might satisfy his passions and
follow his mistress. His mother discovered his intention and tried to intercept him. Under pretense of going to say farewell to a friend who was about to put
to sea, he led her out by way of a little chapel, and
while she was kneeling there in prayer for his redemp-
tion, he slipped away and caught a ship for Italy.

> O'er desert wild, o'er mountain high,
>   A Wanderer I chose to be,
> A wretched soul condemned to die,
>   Still mother's prayers have followed me, . . .
> Have followed me the whole world thro'.[1]

At last her "hopes in this world were accomplished,"
her prayers were answered and her son was saved from
his sins. He was met in the way by Jesus, who stopped
the bier on which his soul was being carried, and said
to him, "Young man, I say unto thee, Arise." And
he that was spiritually dead, sat up and began to speak.
And he gave him back to his mother. "One thing,"
said she, "there was for which I desired to linger for
awhile in this life, that I might see thee a Christian before I died. My God hath done this more abundantly,
that I now see thee, withal, despising earth's happiness,
become His servant." Of his mother's prayers that he
should become a Christian, he writes, "God refused

[1] By permission of The Rodeheaver, Hall-Mack Co., Winona Lake, Ind.

her what she prayed for then, that he might give her what she prayed for always."

> He turned my darkness into light,
>   This blessed Christ of Calvary,
> I'll praise His name both day and night,
>   That mother's prayers have followed me.
> Have followed me the whole world thro'[2]

Mother, would you repossess your son and save him from ruin at the hands of evil companions? Then pray and plan that he shall meet Jesus in the way he goes. Christ alone can put you in full possession of him and make of him the fulfilment of your dearest dreams and the realization of your fondest hopes.

YOUNG MAN, I SAY UNTO THEE, ARISE

In the third place, Jesus has something to say to the son who is dead to mother's hopes, deaf to her prayers, and blind to her tears: "Young man, I say unto thee, Arise." But these words go for naught if the one to whom they are addressed refuses to admit that he is on the downward way. A man cannot be helped up spiritually if he refuses to admit that he has fallen. Christ cannot save a man who refuses to admit that he is a lost sinner. The very first step toward newness of life is to admit that one is in need of renewal.

However, something more is required of a young man who would come to an upright position spiritually: he must have an earnest desire to get up. Just as the seed must respond to the coaxing of soil, sun, and showers, even so must the soul respond to the wooings of

[2]By permission of The Rodeheaver, Hall-Mack Co., Winona Lake, Ind.

the Saviour. Until there has grown up in the heart
of a sinner a desire to be saved, there is no hope of his
spiritual recovery. He must go further. He must be
willing to submit himself to the One who is able to
save. Here is a condition of spiritual recovery that
cannot be omitted. Notice how the Psalmist David
came to an upright position spiritually after he had fallen headlong into heinous sin. First, he admitted his
sin: "I acknowledge my transgressions: and my sin
is ever before me." The next thing he did was to submit his case to the One who was able to cleanse him:
"Wash me throughly from mine iniquity, and cleanse
me from my sin." Once we realize that our health is
failing, we will, if we are wise, submit our case to a
competent physician. And once we realize that we are
sinners, we will submit our souls to the Saviour.

But he who would come to an upright position spiritually must not only admit that he is a sinner and submit his soul to the Saviour, he must also commit himself
to the conditions prescribed. A man may admit that he
is ailing physically; he may submit his case to a competent physician; and yet be unwilling to commit himself wholeheartedly to the conditions prescribed for his
recovery. Few of us do, especially if the treatment is
severe and requires much self-denial and discipline. But
just as the health of the patient depends upon his willingness to commit himself to the conditions prescribed
by the physician, so the spiritual recovery of the soul
depends upon the willingness of the sinner to commit
himself to the conditions prescribed by the Saviour.
Naaman knew and admitted that he was a leper. And
when he was told that there was a man in Israel re-

puted to be able to cure the deadly disease, he submitted his case to him. But when the man of God prescribed a simple remedy, he was angry and unwilling to commit himself to the conditions of the cure. He stalked out of the prophet's presence with his leprosy still upon him. However, he had not gone far before he decided that since he had taken the trouble to travel far to submit his case to him who was reputed to be able to heal, it was foolish not to commit himself to the conditions prescribed. Therefore, he turned back and in full obedience committed himself to the conditions prescribed by the prophet, and was made whole again. Even so it will be with a sinner.

Life is little better than a funeral march until the procession is met and halted by Jesus. Young man, would you be delivered from the clutch of evil companions? Would you be alive to mother's hopes? Would you rise up from your spiritual decease? Then hear these words of the Master, "Young man, I say unto thee, Arise." In response to the call of Christ, sit up, stand up, and straighten up to the full stature of your manhood! He alone is able to break the power of reigning sin and give you back to your mother to become the answer to her prayers, the fulfilment of her dearest dreams, and the realization of her fondest hopes.

XII

BLESSED BE MOTHER

Her children arise up, and call her blessed; her husband also, and
he praiseth her.—PROVERBS 31:28.

I

There is a homely proverb which declares, "You can
find out all you want to know about a boy or a girl by
learning what he or she thinks of mother." This is
only half the truth: you can find out all you want to
know about a mother as well by learning what her
children think of her. Ordinarily a mother gets about
what she deserves in the way of praise or blame. Praise
or want of it is just as indicative of a mother's character
as it is of the conduct of her children. One of the best
proofs that a mother has made a success of a most
difficult task is to be found in the praise her children
bestow. The mother who would have her children "arise
up, and call her blessed" must be a blessed mother. She
must merit their praise.

VIRTUE

What, then, do we find out about this particular
mother by discovering what her children think of her?
Certainly we have a right to expect that she possessed
qualities of character worthy of praise. In this we are
not disappointed. From her son's description we learn
that she was a woman of virtue. "Who can find a
virtuous woman? for her price is far above rubies. The
heart of her husband doth safely trust in her, ...

Many daughters have done virtuously, but thou excellest them all."

No true son has any respect or praise for any other than a virtuous woman; and no woman without it need ever expect that her sons, or the sons of other women will rise up and call her blessed. I was a frequent visitor in a home where the mother's name was never mentioned. I supposed that she was dead until a relative of the family told me the sad story of her unfaithfulness, and final desertion to take up life with another man in a distant city. Then I knew why her name never passed the lips of her husband or her children. She lacked virtue, the first quality of character in a mother that merits the blessing of her children and the praise of her husband.

INDUSTRY

In the second place, from what the children thought of their mother we learn that she was a woman of industry: She worketh willingly with her hands. She eateth not the bread of idleness. She accepted the full responsibility of her office. She was no spendthrift nor gadabout. She was the sort of woman in whose possession her husband's purse found protection. Her industry was not like that of many modern mothers—a job or a career outside the home. She was busy making a home for her children.

Here is a lesson indolent wives and irresponsible mothers would do well to learn. The devil still finds work for idle hands to do. That is one reason many women are given to deviltry today—they are eating the bread of idleness. Science and invention have furnished the modern housekeeper with so many time-saving devices that she has more time on her hands than she knows how to use wisely. A man must lose some of his respect for the woman he calls his wife if she delegates all her duties to servants, while he wears his life out trying to make enough money to keep her in idleness and luxury. My mother, besides being nurse, cook, and housekeeper, spun the yarn, knit stockings and made clothing for a family of ten; and still found time to wear out a Bible perusing its pages. But many a modern mother hires a housekeeper, a nurse for the children, and buys the family wardrobe ready made, and withal is unable to find time to read the Bible or to go to church. What will her children have to say about her? Will they, in the days that are to come, rise up and call her blessed? Not likely. She will get what she deserves.

LOVE

The third quality of character revealed by the praise of this mother's children was that she was both loving and lovable. Proof of this is found in the fact that she gave herself to her family in a labor of love. "She riseth also while it is yet night, and giveth meat to her household." She was no mere servant in the house, given to cooking and housekeeping; she was a home-maker. It was for the future welfare of her children and not for their immediate comfort that she lived, labored, and loved.

One day I listened to the conversation of two mothers. One of them said: "I deny myself for the sake of my children. I feel that my first duty is to them."

She lived and labored for her children and was loved. The other mother replied: "I never allow my children to interfere with my pleasure or comfort. I go and come when I please." She lived for herself,—as though her children were not; and she was not loved. She would never see the day when her children would rise up and call her blessed.

Moreover, the love of this ancient mother was revealed in the tender tone of her voice: "In her tongue is the law of kindness." Blessed is the mother who has learned the fine art of the tender tone of voice. Some mothers never speak until exasperated, then they utter words that stir up strife. To Christ's "If thy right eye offend thee, pluck it out, . . . and if thy right hand offend thee, cut it off." If thy tongue offend thee, or another, cut it off and cast it from thee, should be added. "The tongue is a little member, and boasteth great things. Behold, how great a matter a little fire kindleth! And the tongue is a fire, a world of iniquity: so is the tongue among our members, that it defileth the whole body, and setteth on fire the course of nature; and it is set on fire of hell. . . . The tongue can no man tame; it is an unruly evil, full of deadly poison." But in her tongue was the law of kindness.

WISDOM

In the fourth place, from the praise of her children we learn that she was a woman of wisdom. "She openeth her mouth with wisdom." "Wise wives work wonders with their winsome ways." A labor of love, tenderness of tone, and gentleness of hand are not sufficient to make a mother worthy of her children's praise. These qualities may do much harm if they are not governed by wisdom. Ignorant devotion may ruin children. Too much tenderness and an over amount of anxiety may enfeeble them and make them selfish and self-centered. Professor Gaines, in his book, *Guiding a Growing Life,* says, "What would become of some children if they did not have the power to resist some of the instruction which their fond, foolish parents wish to give them."

The mother who merits the praise of her children is one who knows when to speak, what to say, and how to say it. The mother who opens her mouth to give a command or to declare a decision, and then allows herself to be wheedled into changing her mind, has not opened her mouth with wisdom or won the respect of her children.

RELIGION

In the fifth place, from what this mother's children said of her, we learn that she was a religious woman: "a woman that feareth the Lord." In a very large measure this fact accounts for the praise which her children bestowed; for "a woman that feareth the Lord, she shall be praised." Here, too, is the secret of the saying, "She looketh well to the ways of her household." She had learned to look well to her own ways before she undertook to look well to the ways of her children. Alas, that so many modern mothers do not show any concern for their ways or for the ways of their children. She is a sadly deluded mother who thinks that she can go the way of the world and have her children go the way of the Lord. Yet, that is the foolish supposition of many mothers today. That father's forsake God and the church and become worldly has ceased to be a wonder. But wonder of wonders that mothers should become worldly and irreligious!

The power of a mother to determine the character of her children is beyond calculation. A murderess mothered Nero; and a vain and irreligious woman gave birth to the profligate Lord Byron. On the other hand, a praying Hannah mothered Samuel, and a pious Susanna gave birth to John Wesley. Not all great mothers have had great sons; but all great sons have had great mothers.

A mother should be a Christian because of what Christianity has done for womanhood in general and for motherhood in particular. Of all the changes wrought by the coming of Christ, none has been more significant than the change in the position of woman. Before his coming woman was thought of lightly, and regarded as the inferior and the servant of man. "How low her estate, how pitiable her plight, how degraded her condition without Christ." But ever since that starlit night that Mary "brought forth her firstborn son, and wrapped him in swaddling clothes, and laid him in a manger; because there was no room for them in the inn," womanhood has been ennobled, motherhood dignified, and babyhood glorified. From the hill country of Judea a voice was heard announcing to the world the proclamation of woman's emancipation: "He hath regarded the low estate of his handmaiden: for, behold, from henceforth all generations shall call me blessed. For he that is mighty hath done to me great things."

Moreover, a mother should be a Christian because of what Christ has done for childhood. The child occupied a place of little concern in the affairs of men until Christ came. But ever since the day he took a little child, set him in the midst and exalted him to the rank of first citizen of the kingdom of heaven, the child has occupied a central place in society.

"MOTHER O'MINE"

From the foregoing it is evident that here was a mother who merited the praise of her children, and they performed their part well. "Her children arise up, and call her blessed; her husband also, and he praiseth her." But what about that "mother o'mine"? The portrait of this mother of old is but a counterpart of your mother and mine. And since our mothers emulate the virtues of this mother of another era, we would do well to follow the example of her children: rise up and call them blessed.

The greatest blessing that children can bestow upon mother is to become the fulfilment of her fondest hopes, and the realization of her dearest dreams. Herein is her biggest and best wages and the occasion of the sweetest pleasure that earth can yield. She is "bound up in a bundle of life" with us. Her prayers are for us and her hopes are in us. If we would bless her name or honor her memory, we must live nobly and well. For it is not the praise of our lips, but the praise of our lives that brings satisfaction and peace to her heart.

In the words of an unknown poet she speaks to us today,

> Do you know that your soul is of my soul such a part
> That you seem to be fiber and core of my heart?
> None other can pain me as you, Son, can do;
> None other can praise me or please me as you.
> Remember, the world will be quick with its blame
> If shadow or stain ever darken your name.
>
> "Like mother, like son," is a saying so true
> This world will judge largely of mother by you.
> Be this then your task,—if task it shall be—
> To force this proud world to do homage to me.
> Be sure it will say when its verdict is won,
> "She reaps as she sowed. This man is her son."

XIII

WHAT CHRIST EXPECTS OF A CHRISTIAN

Why call ye me, Lord, Lord, and do not the things which I say?—LUKE 6:46.

I

This morning we confront ourselves with the second in a series of topics prepared for a program of "Visitation Evangelism," namely, "What Christ Expects of a Christian." The theme is amply set forth and fully comprehended in Luke 6:46: "Why call ye me, Lord, Lord, and do not the things which I say?"

In the first place, the text makes it clear that Christ expects a Christian to accept his Word as the rule and guide of faith and conduct and honestly endeavor to do what he says. But when we start with a premise like that we are at once confronted with something very exacting and difficult. For example, Christ said, "Love your enemies, bless them that curse you, do good to them that hate you, and pray for them which despitefully use you, and persecute you."

In a day when war has been declared upon us by three treacherous, malicious, and hateful enemies, it is an audacious thing for a minister to stand up and confront his people with the premise that Christ expects a Christian to do what he says when he says, "Love your enemies. . . ." Yet that is just what I am daring to do; for I preach Christ, and the Christ I preach said, "Love your enemies, bless them that curse you, do good to them that hate you, and pray for them which despitefully use you, and persecute you." That is a hard saying to front, and the more so today because of what happened on December 7, 1941, at Pearl Harbor.

A short time after the attack by Japan, a rather shocking thing appeared on the front page of the *Charleston Gazette.* The paper had blocked the brief news item so that it would not escape the eyes of the reader. The news item had as its caption,

MARINES DECLARE "OPEN SEASON" ON JAPANESE

"Los Angeles, California, January 8,
'Jap hunting licenses issued here.   Open season now.   No limit.'
That was the sign that went up today outside the United States Marines' recruiting station in the federal building.   Fifty youths lined up to apply for the licenses."

That was all that was said, but it was enough. It adequately expressed the state of mind of the marines. After Pearl Harbor, one cannot much blame the marines. I suspect that the epigrammatic statement posted by the marines expressed the feeling and attitude of multitudes of Americans toward the Japanese; and that makes it the more ominous. We are in danger of becoming a nation of haters and headhunters.

In the face of world circumstances, dare we admonish ourselves to obey Christ when he says, "Love your enemies"?   We profess to believe that Christ spoke with divine authority, but in a time like this we are inclined to live as though he need not be taken seriously when he said, "Love your enemies . . . and pray for them. . . ." The trouble with all too many of us is that we are not willing to become Christians on Christ's terms. We want to be Christians on our own terms, with the result that we make a gesture at being Christian on Sunday, and then on Monday revert to the pagans we really are. Mr. Massingham, late editor of the *London Nation,* said: "I am fond of Jesus Christ, but I never make any effort to do what he tells me to do. Somehow this world has slipped out of his control; and yet, if it knew, it would find in him a happy and easy way of life."

In stating his case, Mr. Massingham stated yours and mine. Many of us are fond of Jesus Christ, but we never make any serious efforts to do what he says. We may not publicly deny nor openly reject any particular thing he said, but, what is worse, it often happens that our lips profess a faith which our lives belie. For when in the course of events we come upon some difficult saying of his, one that cuts right straight across our selfish way, as does this one: "Love your enemies . . . ," we wilfully dodge it or seek to explain it away.

Though unschooled in the art of interpreting the Scriptures, yet the average layman has become a veritable genius in the art of exegesis. He can take almost any plain, straightforward, unmistakable statement of Jesus and by punctuation, accentuation, interpretation, or clever explanation denature it until it fits very nicely into a selfish way of life. We need to be reminded that when God said, "This is my beloved son; hear ye him," he was admonishing us to accept the plain and obvious meaning of Christ's words, and to do so without "hesitation, mental reservation, or secret evasion of mind." Mary the mother of Jesus gave a bit of wise counsel which we would do well to hear and heed. There was a wedding in Cana of Galilee, and Jesus and his mother were there. Apparently the number of guests exceeded the expectation of the host, and the refreshments ran out, creating an embarrassing situation. This was brought to the attention of Mary who, mother-like, went and told Jesus. From that interview she came back with this significant bit of counsel, "Whatever he tells you to do, do it."

Well do I remember when I was wrestling with a call to the ministry. I formulated arguments and offered excuses for not doing what had become to me the explicit will of God. I argued that the material for which God was calling was too ordinary and that there were many others who would serve his purpose better. Then it was that my mother swept away all arguments, leaving me defenseless when she said: "Son, whatever he tells you to do, do it. For he that knoweth the will of God and doeth it not shall be beaten with many stripes." And when I find it difficult to obey my Lord today I can still hear my mother say, "Son, whatever he tells you to do, do it."

That should characterize the attitude of every Christian today. If Christians had taken that attitude toward the teachings of Christ, the foundations of civilization would not now be crumbling. For said Christ, "Whosoever heareth these sayings of mine, and doeth them, I will liken him unto a wise man, which built his house upon a rock: and the rain descended, and the floods came, and the winds blew, and beat upon that house; and it fell not: for it was founded upon a rock. And every one that heareth these sayings of mine, and doeth them not, shall be likened unto a foolish man, which built his house upon the sand: and the rain descended, and the floods came, and the winds blew, and beat upon that house; and it fell: and great was the fall of it." Because we have been hearing his sayings and doing them not, today these words are being fulfilled in our ears and before our eyes.

II

In the second place, Christ expects a Christian to acknowledge him as Lord and to be obedient to his will. Here again it is perfectly clear that when we start with a premise like that we are confronted with serious difficulty. For Christ said, "Not every one that saith unto me, Lord, Lord, shall enter into the kingdom of heaven; but he that doeth the will of my Father who is in heaven." "Ye call me Master and Lord: and ye say well; for so I am." "But why call ye me, Lord, Lord, and do not the things which I say?" You see, the Lordship of Jesus implies stewardship of the believer; and obedience to his will implies servitude of the disciple. To call him Lord, and refuse to be his steward; to call him Master, and refuse to be his servant is to fall woefully short of what Christ expects of a Christian.

In knighthood days, for self-protection, it was the custom of men to swear allegiance to some powerful lord. They would kneel at his feet, place their hands in his, take an oath of allegiance, become his men, and then rise up and go forth to do his will. Christ expects as much of us. On becoming Christians, we took an oath of allegiance to our Lord; we became his children. But alas! Either by lip or life, in our character or conduct, we often deny the Lordship of Jesus, saying, "We will not have this man rule over us."

To be sure, objections will arise in the minds of men when a minister speaks so plainly and pleads so earnestly that Christians become obedient to the word and will of Christ. One of the very first objections which come to rebellious minds is that if Christians were to go about taking Christ at his word and doing his will, they would be labeled religious fanatics. And most of us fear that epithet as we do the plague. But Christians must have the sort of courage the early Christians possessed, the courage and the consecration to be called "fools for Christ's sake." "We are fools for Christ's sake," said the Apostle Paul; "but we are wise in Christ."

But of one thing I am not uneasy, namely, that Christians shall overdo their obedience to the will of Christ. I see no evidence whatever that Christians are in any danger of throwing caution to the wind in their zeal to do what Christ expects of them. The danger is that they shall become so cautious and so calculating that they shall secretly condemn Jesus as an impractical idealist and lay aside his gospel as something "too high and good for human nature's daily food."

To do what Christ says and to be obedient to his will is not easy. Whoever said it was! Do you think it was easy for Christ when in the garden of Gethsemane he faced the agony of the cross, praying, "O

my Father, if it be possible, let this cup pass from me."
Yet he closed that prayer with these words of self-
surrender, "Nevertheless, not my will, but thine, be
done." To that attitude toward the will of our Lord
we must come. This is no easy gospel. Indeed, this is
no time for an easy gospel. The time has come when
we need to hear some plain, positive preaching. For
that reason it is not my purpose to preach a gospel that
will encourage self-complacency. It is my intention to
dig about the roots of your religion and not merely to
decorate the branches of your faith with a little arti-
ficial fruit. Therefore, I make bold to say that Christ
expects a Christian to accept his word and obey his will.

Think of a minister in a day like this daring to
stand up and admonish Christians to do what Christ
said and to be obedient to his will! Yet, if there is
anything that these dreadful days are making clear to
our hard hearts and dull minds, it is that we must
become the servants of a loving Lord or the abject
slaves of a hateful Hitler. In spite of the fact that
we are at war, the need today is that Christians every-
where shall acknowledge the Lordship of Christ, do
what he says, and faithfully and courageously obey
his will. For what will it avail if in days like these
we lip the name of our Lord while our lives give the
lie to all that our lips profess. "Why call ye me Lord,
Lord, and do not the things which I say?"

III

In the third place, Christ expects Christians to walk
in his way. "I am the way," said he, "follow me." "I
have given you an example," said he, "do as I have
done."

When I was a lad in the one-room school, I learned to write by trying to imitate a copy that had been set by the teacher. As I began close up to the copy, the first line of my work was not too bad,—there was none of my poor work intervening. But the second line was not so good, and the third was less legible. The farther away I got from the copy the more imperfect was my writing. By the time I reached the bottom of one of those long foolscap sheets of paper I had grown careless and was copying my own imperfections, and the final result was a sight to behold. You would understand what I mean if you should undertake to read anything that I have written! The remedy for the poor work which I had done was to get back close to the copy and start all over again.

This is a homely parable of the Christian's failure to be more like his Lord. Between him and the matchless man of Galilee stands his own imperfections which he copies, vainly thinking that he is following Christ. The remedy for his mistake and pitiable failure is to get back to Christ and follow his example and walk in his way.

Because Christians have not walked the way of Christ, they are not impressing the world as the early Christians did. They made such a profound impression on the political, social, moral, and spiritual life of their day that they were accused of turning the world upside down. And so they were! And the reason for it was that they did what Christ said; they obeyed his will, they walked in his way. The record of Christian history gives abundant proof that the sort of Christianity that has impressed the world and won respect has been the kind that has done what the Lord has said instead of being content to say what he has done.

I would not leave the impression that the kind of Christianity which says what the Lord has done is not important. It is. One of the things, and not the least, that Christ expects of a Christian is, "Go, . . . tell how great things the Lord has done for thee." But the sort of Christians needed today are those who do what he has said as well as say what he has done. If Christians would impress the world they must prove what he has done by doing what he has said. They must be obedient to his will and walk in his way. For it is the Christian's walk, and not his talk, that counts with the world. We might gather here in this sanctuary Sunday after Sunday and sing,

> My Jesus, I love Thee, I know Thou art mine,
> For Thee all the follies of sin I resign;
> My gracious Redeemer, my Saviour art Thou;
> If ever I loved Thee, my Jesus, 'tis now.

But unless we go forth to do the things he said, to obey his will and walk in his way, our worship will be as meaningless as sounding brass or clanging cymbal.

We know very well that the word, the will, and the way of Christ is the only way to peace on earth and good will among men. If Christians the world around had been doing what Christ expects of Christians, this horrible war would have been averted. And if Christians today the world around would begin to do what Christ expects of Christians, they could coin the present calamity into capital for Christ and turn this wicked war torn world back to God. They would hasten the day when "Every knee shall bow," and "every tongue shall confess" that he is "King of kings, and Lord of lords." They would usher in the day when together we could truly say,

> All hail the power of Jesus' name!
>   Let angels prostrate fall;
> Bring forth the royal diadem,
>   And crown Him Lord of all.